DRUG ADDICTION

Learn About It Before Your Kids Do

Pierre Andre, M.D.

Health Communications, Inc.
Pompano Beach, Florida

Pierre Andre
Nova University
Fort Lauderdale, Florida

Reprint Permission Acknowledgments

Page 16: Reprinted with permission by **The Miami Herald.**

Page 103: From' "Appendix A' 800-Cocaine Research Questionnaire from **800-COCAINE** by Mark S. Gold, M.D. Copyright ©1984 by Mark S. Gold. Reprinted by permission of Bantam Books, Inc. All rights reserved.

Page 117: Most of the Cocaine Treatment Facilities addresses were taken from : Appendix B of the book **Cocaine** by Roger Weiss, M.D. and Steven Mirin, M.D. Reprint with permission of the authors and the American Psychiatric Press.

Library of Congress Cataloging-in-Publication Data

Andre, Pierre, 1946-
Drug addiction.

Bibliography: p.
1. Cocaine habit — United States — Prevention.
2. Cocaine habit — Treatment. 3. Youth — United States — Drug use — Prevention. I. Title
HV5810.A62 1987 363.2'93 87-21205
ISBN 0-932194-58-3

ISBN 0-932194-58-3

Published by Health Communications, Inc.
1721 Blount Road
Pompano Beach, Florida 33069

Foreword

The epidemic of cocaine abuse in the United States in the 1980s strained traditional treatment resources — not just from the point of view of numbers, but conceptually as well. The medical community, as well as the media, had looked on cocaine as a relatively benign recreational drug associated with rock stars, professional athletes and other rich who lived life in the fast lane. Even in the official psychiatric nomenclature there was no diagnosis of "cocaine addiction", only "abuse".

We soon learned, however, that cocaine was among the most addictive of drugs. The rapidly increasing procession of strung-out people and burned-out lives from all strata of society taught us that lesson. The 800-COCAINE National Helpline not only directed millions to treatment resources, but documented the medical, psychological, social, occupational and legal problems associated with cocaine use. We documented the rapid course of cocaine addiction and the desperate depression and cocaine craving associated with chronic use and withdrawal from cocaine.

The availability of "crack" — the more potent and cheaper form of smokeable cocaine free-base — from 1985 on upped the ante for cocaine users. We in Florida became particularly aware of the problems of crack and began to see even more intense degrees of addiction. Crack became all too available to adolescents in schools all across America, and teenage crack abuse became a major public health problem.

But we also began to understand more about cocain addiction. The White House focused public awareness on t the disease of cocaine addiction, particularly among teenagers

Medical research began to uncover the biochemical effec of cocaine on the brain's pleasure centers, which account fo cocaine's addictive properties. Our group and others ha begun to develop medicines to reduce the torment o withdrawing from cocaine while allowing successful treatme interventions to take place. Industry is learning how to identi the cocaine addict in the workplace and guide him or her t treatment resources. Alcoholics Anonymous and Narcotics Anonymous are integrating cocaine addicts into their self-help recovery programs.

It was against this background of increasing understanding and development of effective treatments for cocaine addiction that the Fair Oaks Hospital Group established a Fellowship in the area of addiction several years ago. This gives psychiatrists just completing their training the opportunity to develop expertise in the complex field of addiction. The Fellow must learn about pharmacology and detoxification, as well as working with individuals, groups and families. He or she must learn the disease concept of addiction and the 12-Step Recovery Program. In addition, the Fellow learns to treat the multiple medical and psychiatric problems which develop in the "dual diagnosis" addicted patient. Above all, the Fellow learns to integrate the different skills and viewpoints needed for successful treatment planning.

It has been my pleasure to have Pierre Andre, M.D., as Addiction Fellow at Fair Oaks Hospital at Boca/Delray during the academic year 1986-1987. Dr. Andre has approached his Fellowship as a professional and a gentleman. He has participated in our clinical programs as well as our research on the neurochemistry of cocaine addiction. His open-minded curiosity has led to the clear and concise integration of the multifaceted aspects of cocaine addiction and its treatment, which is presented in this book. In ***Drug Addiction: Learn About It Before Your Kids Do*** Dr. Andre has presented the disease of addiction in a concise manner. I think the non-professional reader to whom this book is aimed will get a very human feel for the torment and struggle of addicted individuals and their families, as well as the very real possibilities for professional help available.

Irl Extein, M.D.
Medical Director
Fair Oaks Hospital
at Boca/Delray,
Delray Beach, Florida

Preface

With decreased price and increased availability, cocaine is now found everywhere from Beverly Hills and Wall Street to the inner cities.

The era of democratization of cocaine use has become a serious public health concern, a major economic burden and a threat to our children.

The primary purpose of this book is to educate the public about cocaine addiction, its prevention and treatment, and drug dependence in general.

All characters in this book are fictional and any similarity to any person living or dead is purely coincidental.

Acknowledgments

I am grateful to my colleague and friend, Terri B. Collins, A.C.S.W., for her substantial contribution to the second part of this book: Importance of Family Therapy. Ms. Collins is the Director of Social Services at Fair Oaks Hospital.

I wish to thank my colleague and friend, Dr. Charles Norris, and the entire Fair Oaks team, particularly Doctors Irl Extein, Mark Gold, David Gross, Carter Pottash, William Rafuls, William Rea, Eric Ressner, Dean Rotondo and Anthony Yacona, for their constant support.

Last, but definitely not the least, my words of appreciation go to my wife Natalie, who has been my typist, secretary and chief adviser for the past fifteen years, for without her assistance my task would have been extremely difficult.

Epigraph

The World Health Organization defines drug dependence as "a state, psychic or also sometimes physical, resulting from interaction between a living organism and a drug, and characterized by behavioral and other responses that always include a compulsive desire or need to use the drug on a continuous basis in order to experience its effects and/or avoid the discomfort of its absence."

The process of cocaine addiction illustrates perfectly this definition of drug dependence.

— WHO Expert Committee on
Addiction-Producing Drugs,
13th Report Publication 273
World Health Organization
Technical Report Series, Geneva, 1964.

Dedication

Dedicated to Dorothy Pullman and in memory of Esau and Bethie Andre and Paul Pullman

Contents

PART I
Cocaine Addiction and Treatment

1

Hooked on Drugs

Born and brought up in a small town in Wisconsin, Peter was the youngest of three children. His mother was a school teacher, his father a pharmacist. His older brother and sister were both successful. They went straight to college after high school, went into professions and settled down with families in their hometown.

Peter was the baby and developed some of that position's traditional irresponsibility. He was a lukewarm scholar, but does not recall any great shame attached to his mediocrity. His family was fairly relaxed, its members busy with their own itineraries.

Sometimes this had a negative result in that he lacked guidance. One incident in particular stands out in his memory. When he was 12, he had become quite friendly with two brothers who were strangers to his family. He was intrigued by their activities, which were exciting and different from his own humdrum habits. Their parents seemed almost non-existent, coming home late and not always sober; the brothers were on their own.

They managed to find many creative ways to fill their time — hunting with sticks and stones, breaking up bushes and small trees in lots both vacant and occupied, writing dirty words in abandoned houses, etc. Peter went along with them, not judging what they were doing until all three were caught methodically butchering a farmer's prize hens. Although Peter was more of an on-looker than an active participant, the horrified reactions of his family quickly squashed his stray into anti-social behavior. His family kept a closer eye on him for a while, but eventually they returned to their own activities while Peter continued on his essentially rudderless development.

He did learn one thing from this experience: Mores depend not on what's right, but on what the majority is doing. He remembers as an adolescent feeling strongly that his misadventure at age 12 was due to following a minority. From then on he resolved to follow the crowd. He wondered how right and wrong were delineated by philosophers. Even now he feels unsure of how one can come to an independent conclusion about morality.

There was no history of drug or alcohol abuse in his immediate family, although his father and sister both smoked moderately.

Wisconsin had two drinking age limits: 18 for beer, 21 for hard liquor. The result was a juvenile emphasis on beer drinking, and a "pecking order" of status for types of alcohol and types of IDs. Sixteen and seventeen year olds tried to get false 18-year-old IDs, and 18- to 20-year-olds tried for false 21-year-old IDs. Many who might not otherwise drink did so because it was expected, especially in bars which were a normal place for young people to congregate. Only a staunch nonconformist (or a teetotaler) would order a soda while socializing in a bar, and few, outside of members of some religious sects, refused to step into bars. Alcohol consumption was pervasive, although not always heavy.

Drinking, therefore, was the norm, and Peter did not abuse alcohol. He does remember several "benders" when friends dared each other to drink heavily. He recalls no heavy drinking by himself at any time, then or now.

He finished high school in 1964 and drifted around in menial jobs "finding himself" for one year. Then he joined the

Army just before a draft would have been inevitable, and was stationed in Germany. While classmates were being attacked and destroyed in Vietnam, he sat around and chatted until coffee breaks at 10:00, chatted some more until lunch, and wore away the afternoon similarly occupied in a boring routine of clerical work in Southern Germany.

Hemmed in by snow, language barriers and various official and unofficial restraints, he joined the practices of the "flower children" and used marijuana and LSD.

Upon leaving the Army in 1968, he entered the heyday of the *laissez faire* drug culture of the late 60s in New York City. He avoided 'hard' drugs — injected ones — but drifted along with dead end jobs and the handouts of friends till he 'hit bottom'.

One day while in between jobs, he got sick with pneumonia and a high fever. Going to the nearest emergency room, uninsured and penniless, he got brief treatment and was sent on his way with a very high temperature.

Sensing that his condition was more serious than the careless ER crew had implied, he called some straight-living relatives in the area. They nursed him back to health, and he realized that he could well have died. This shook him up so deeply that he started back on the road to an orthodox lifestyle, complete with education.

He went on to college and a comfortable family life. Until recently, his only vestige was a 'medicinal' use of marijuana when under stress and, as always, an occasional social use of alcohol.

Basically he attributes his early adulthood drug abuse to that era's influences, and his survival to his own inner strength of character. This is what makes his recent addiction to cocaine so bewildering. He assumed, having been strong enough to overcome drugs in his early twenties, he could "take it or leave it" when he experimented recently.

Peter is now a 40-year-old corporate executive in an investment firm. He is bright, articulate, self-confident. He has earned the respect of everyone from the president to the janitor. In ten years, he has already moved up the corporate ladder to become the youngest vice president of his company.

He lives in an upper middle class suburban community. He has been married to Jenny for 16 years, and they have three young children. He has prestige, status, love, money and an energetic, happy family.

He was in the midst of financial and professional success, when a friend introduced him to cocaine at a party. At first, he hesitated but reluctantly he decided to try a snort. Why not?! Everyone was doing it! After all, morality is based on the majority's opinions and habits, just as he had believed as an adolescent. What's wrong with a little experimentation? To his surprise he felt the lift in a matter of seconds. Delighted, he graciously volunteered for a few more snorts. He called home to let his wife know that he would be home later than expected. The reason: he was discussing new business ventures with a few associates.

In the following months he found himself snorting two to three times a week. He didn't wait too long to move to free base and in a year he entered the Big League of crack. By that time he was totally possessed and obsessed! He was thinking about it, dreaming about it, craving it, using it, constantly. Before work he would have some to get a lift to start the day. During lunch hour he would get some to relieve the pressure of the day, a reminiscence of the alcoholic who always finds a reason for booze, a cause to celebrate. In good times and bad! In time of great successes and in time of dismal failures! In time of war and in time of peace!

2

Meaning of Addiction

Addiction involves three factors:

compulsion,
loss of control,
and continued use in spite of adverse consequences

Addiction creates a powerful motivational state overwhelming all other motivations including self-preservation. Animal studies have demonstrated that animals will prefer cocaine over available food and water, and animals have been known to die of starvation while self-reinforcing cocaine.

In humans the compulsion is somewhat similar. The addict is totally powerless, his compulsive use of drugs becomes his main goal and everything else is secondary: his health, his family, his job. He has become the slave of a chemical.

To describe this compulsion, I like to recall this picture drawn by Dr. Harley Thompson, a specialist in substance abuse treatment: (Fair Oaks Grand Rounds 9/17/86: *Addiction & the Family).*

Let's imagine the effect of being deprived of water. Imagine being in a desert country where water is a high priority and that one of the effects of breaking the law is to be condemned to not drinking water, which is tantamount to a death sentence.

Let's say you are branded with something that says that you are not to drink water and anyone who gives you water is subject to criminal charges himself. It would take only three to four days until you would die, unless you got water. So you will be pretty desperate by the end of the second or third day. You would probably be willing to take the risk of losing your life or being thrown in jail to gain access to water. There would probably be a black market from which you could obtain water, paying exorbitant amounts of money. You might be found sneaking into people's backyards and putting your mouth to the spigot, etc.

You could say that water is necessary but drugs are not. To the addict, that is consciously an acceptable statement, but below the level of consciousness, operating directly on the appetite system, the hypothalamus and so on, the brain is saying something entirely different. In a sense drugs become necessary and in adapting to drugs, the brain develops a tolerance which results in severe rebound effects when they are stopped. Drugs create needs that are more compelling than the desire for water, food, sex. No matter what the addict believes on a conscious level, his brain sends out signals that result in compulsive behaviors. This is another reason why the conscious thoughts and words of an addicted person are not as important as the actions that he engages in. Thus the saying, "When the addict talks, look at his feet, not his lips."

In its devastating course addiction finally leads to at least one of the three outcomes:

death
jail
psychiatric or rehabilitation center.

Death

Drugs can kill easily; the toxic side effects, the physical and emotional strains can cause problems ranging from heart attack, respiratory arrest, seizures, stroke, suicide. You don't have to "hit bottom" to be a victim; bottom can come up and hit you. We have seen healthy professionals (athletes and entertainers) killed by drugs in the midst of their professional careers. In summary, the causes of death can be physical (heart attacks, stroke, respiratory failure), accidental (car accidents) or emotional (suicide).

Jail

If you use drugs, the compulsion is so powerful that you will do whatever it takes to get them. If you are not rich, you may steal, prostitute yourself, even kill in order to support the habit. Any of these options can win you a free ticket to jail.

Rehabilitation Programs

These give the addict the opportunity to bring his "chemical insanity" under control. They are the only feasible options for the cocaine addict and come in a variety of approaches and arrangements, including inpatient settings and/or outpatient recovery centers.

3

Types of Drug Addicts

This society has become a chemical culture. Children are taught that there is a pill for every pain and discomfort: headache, sore throat, insomnia, fatigue, weight gain, weight loss, depression, anxiety, stress, you name it.

Family medicine cabinets are filled with Tylenol, aspirin, tranquilizers, vitamins, diet pills, pain killers, cough syrups and decongestants.

On television, in newspapers and in magazines, professional athletes and entertainers are seen in advertisements for beer, wine and sleeping pills. Drugs have become symbols of prestige, success, happiness and relaxation. Many young people identify with the fast-paced, hard-driving sound of rock, punk and heavy metal music whose lyrics often encourage drug use, sex and violence.

Traditionally drug addiction was regarded as a problem of the ghettos and inner cities. An addict was seen as a junkie shooting up heroin in an alley. An alcoholic was pictured as a disheveled, old looking man on a street corner, a skid row bum, although less than 5% of alcoholics end up on skid row.

There is now a growing recognition that the drug problem has reached all the layers of society.

An addict can be a housewife popping Valium, Xanax or Ativan pills in order to "cope with daily stresses", drugs often prescribed by a physician.

An addict can be a corporate manager, a lawyer, a school teacher or an air traffic controller snorting cocaine to enhance feelings of competence or to increase alertness and energy.

An addict can be a physician, a nurse or another health professional hooked on narcotics like Demerol or mood-altering drugs.

An addict can be a prostitute busy hustling to support an expensive habit. There is now a new generation of the so-called "cocaine whores" in the street, trading sex for crack.

An addict can be an adolescent who started smoking marijuana or drinking beer for one of several reasons: curiosity, peer pressure, boredom, rebellion against parents or relaxation. Then the use led to abuse and finally to addiction.

An addict can be a Yuppie who discovers that power, prestige, fame and money bring as much stress as failure. There is constant drive and pressure towards better performance for greater achievements. At some point during this competitive race he gets burned out, unable to take this pressure in addition to the daily hassles of details waiting like hungry sharks to be appeased.

Doctor Steven Berglas in "**The Success Syndrome**" describes how one can hit bottom while on the top.

"The 1980s is not the first time that success has been recognized as taking a toll on interpersonal relationships or physical health. The 1950s gave us the proverbial '**Man in the Gray Flannel Suit**', frequently portrayed as success-wracked by ulcers.

"Many who reach **the top** will get the cold beer that Michelob promised along with a host of other rewards. Others get the same rewards and much more than they asked for: they become alcoholics. Many successes who can **hold** their liquor suffer other consequences of The Success Syndrome, ranging from failed careers to destroyed relationships."

For Harold Kushner, the factor that is adversely affecting the quality of many people's life is boredom. (Harold Kushner,

When All You've Ever Wanted Is Not Enough. Summit Books, New York.)

"The affliction which drains so much of the sense of meaning from our lives these days is the disease of boredom. So many of us find our jobs boring, our marriages boring, our friendships and hobbies boring. In pathetic desperation we look for a movie, a vacation trip, an outlet of some sort to lift our lives above the level of the mundane. Some of us will find ourselves doing all sorts of potentially self-destructive things — driving too fast, hang-gliding, white-water rafting, because 'only then do I feel alive'. Some people will turn to drugs in a desperate effort to rise above the emotional flatness of the everyday and learn what it feels like to feel again."

4

What is Crack?

Crack is a deadly, cheap derivative of cocaine, its most destructive, most addictive form.

Coca Plant

The coca plant, Erythroxilon Coca, is a three-foot tall evergreen shrub. It grows at elevations of 1500 to 6000 feet, primarily on the slopes of the Andes Mountains in South America. The plant is not harvested until the vegetation is two to three years old. However, it keeps producing its bulky leaves for the next twenty years. These leaves are removed two to three times a year and are transported by the farmers to the processing plants of the nearest village.

Coca Paste

The leaves are macerated with water, sodium bicarbonate, sulphuric acid and kerosene, transforming it into coca paste.

Cocaine Powder or 'Coke'

Coca paste is treated with a number of chemicals, which may include hydrochloric acid, ammonia, acetone, sulphuric acid, kerosene, ether, calcium and sodium carbonate. This converts it into cocaine hydrochloride, the snowy white powder known as coke.

Crack or Rock

Powdered cocaine mixed with water and baking soda is heated until it is solid. Then it is broken into small whitish grey pebbles known as crack or rock.

Crack is smoked and goes directly from the lungs to the brain, causing a quick "rush" in two to three seconds. The "high" lasts 10 to 15 minutes. Soon after that, the user goes through severe withdrawal, experiencing depression, anxiety and irritability. He may find himself using crack after crack, not to feel good, but to keep from feeling bad.

The impact of crack on a community was starkly described in Lynne Duke's article "Crack" published in the *Miami Herald Tropic Magazine* of April 5, 1987:

"It used to be a neighborhood. Then crack moved in.

". . . Crack is squeezing the life out of an entire community, crowding out normal motivations, killing hopefulness, completely rewriting despair. The fear of the innocent people, the treachery of the guilty ones, the hopelessness of the victims — all have conspired to snuff out much of what once had been pleasant and good.

"Crack isn't like the drug scourges of the past, like heroin in the 1950s, LSD in the 1960s, cocaine tooting in the 1970s. It's as seductive and addictive as any of them, and at least as physically destructive, but it's more plentiful, and its high can come as cheaply as a pint of bourbon. Only you don't sleep this high off when you are finished; you are ravenous for more, right away, and the hunger feeds on itself. It is a macabre courtship, till death do us part."

5

Drugs in the Workplace

When Peter began using cocaine, it was helpful for him at work. He enjoyed a tremendous increase in confidence and self-image. Cocaine first produced a feeling of omnipotence, increased energy and mental sharpness. Peter felt like a salesman ready to 'sell the world'. But in truth he had sold his soul to the devil. After a while he began to pay the price for this confidence building. The side effects of the drug started to surface: depression, lack of motivation, irritability, paranoia.

At the job, his superiors, colleagues and subordinates noticed the change. First of all, his personal appearance began to suffer. He was no longer the clean shaven manager with the pinstripe suit. He lost weight. He looked preoccupied. He seemed anxious. His smile was gone. He was restless. The calm and collected gentleman now had a quick temper, was easily irritable, with a sharp tongue.

Clients began to complain; he started losing business, and with it his confidence. His job performance declined tremendously. He was paranoid, stating that his colleagues wanted his head.

There was the time a client, Christopher, came to discuss his portfolio. Peter and Christopher were long-time acquaintances, moving in the same social circles. Christopher had just separated from his wife of 18 years, and he was on an emotional tightrope. He needed to know what he and his wife were worth financially to prepare for a possible division of assets. He was miserable, but he was also the kind of person who hides his feelings. Deep down Peter may have sensed that Christopher was at the brink emotionally. But Peter was at his own brink. It had been too long, at least four hours, since his last rock, and he was extremely edgy.

A pile of work awaited him, a pile of work was always awaiting him, and Christopher had walked in without an appointment, just as Peter was planning his lunchtime itinerary. (No, he wasn't deciding which restaurant to go to. He was deciding whether to lock his door and close his blinds, an act which could look suspicious, or wait until everyone was out at lunch, which might not happen, or go to a restroom, the undignified alternative which he resorted to all too often. He also thought about which restaurants had the proper kind of stalls, the kind with a single toilet and a locked front door rather than a multi-unit restroom.)

Peter was aware of Christopher's plight, and his own marital stresses may have made him more uncomfortable in the comparison. What if it were Jenny who was divorcing him? But his misery prevented him from feeling any compassion, and he was furious with Christopher for interrupting his plans. Without even fetching Christopher's file, he assured him that he would look up what they were worth, and start laying plans to liquidate their holdings. He treated Christopher as though there was no other bond between them, at a time when Christopher could have used a few strokes.

When Christopher pointed out that he had made this request over the phone three weeks before, but hadn't heard from Peter, Peter blew up. He had no memory of this request, and felt guilty for having neglected it to the point of complete amnesia.

"For God sakes," shouted Peter, "I didn't forget. Don't you see this pile of work in front of me? I've got tons of stuff to do, reports to make, and the new system they've introduced here doesn't make it any easier. Your wife will have to wait. She shouldn't be so money-hungry and you shouldn't be so eager to appease her. What are you, a wimp? Tell her to go stuff it! And leave me alone, I'll get it done!"

Christopher, who was being, as always, meticulous and fair-minded about details, was mortified and embarrassed. Peter's co-workers could not believe their ears. Although there had been several similar outbursts against them, each one had thought he was partially to blame, each one somehow excused Peter. But the customer is always right, and this display against a client, and public criticism of the company itself (the "new system" was over one year old), was too much. While Peter went to lunch, the office buzzed with descriptions of what happened.

When Peter returned, there was an unnatural quiet about the place. He knew he had gone too far, but this did not humble him. He even went so far as to retrieve Christopher's file and place it in his In-Box.

But as the afternoon wore on, and his usual irritability increased, the incident played on his mind. Tony, the newest vice-president in the firm, an energetic, enthusiastic carbon copy of Peter eight years ago, may somehow have had something to do with it. After all, Peter had seen him talking to Christopher after the incident, talking softly and apologetically. Perhaps he was after Peter's position, wanting to eliminate the competition, and was laying the groundwork. Perhaps he had even set him up, sending Christopher in to see him when he knew he would be at his worst.

The illogic of this escaped Peter, even the faint admission that he would be at his worst just before his next 'fix'. He continued to brood about the situation, and never did get to Christopher's file that day.

Problems Associated with Drugs in the Workplace

The intrusion of drugs into the workplace has caused tremendous losses to business due to decrease in productivity, reduced product quality, faulty decisions, high absenteeism, diversion of funds by embezzlement and a high rate of job-related accidents among equipment operators.

The Employees Assistance Program (EAP) was created for treatment of employees affected by alcohol and drug addiction in an attempt to minimize the impact of the problem. Drugs in the workplace threaten all of us. Machinery that is poorly assembled is as dangerous as car brakes that don't work properly. Poor quality goods are disappointments. Factory equipment at the hands of a drug abuser poses a danger to himself and others. A stoned air traffic controller, an intoxicated train engineer, an impaired surgeon jeopardize hundreds of lives.

Today most major corporations have a drug policy which reflects the company's determination to keep a safe work environment. Management is alert to any drastic change in an employee's behavior which suggests drug abuse. Absenteeism, tardiness, repeated sick leave, erratic work performance, highs and lows, frequent mistakes, poor judgment or a high rate of accidents are documented and discussed with the employee. Then EAP counseling may be recommended.

Supervisors should avoid scare tactics, "I'll see to it that you're fired"; moral judgments, "You are a lousy bum, a junkie"; or cover ups, "I don't want to get involved". Those statements are all detrimental to elimination of drugs in the workplace.

Most major companies will not terminate an employee with a drug problem unless he relapses or refuses treatment. After all, it costs less to treat an employee than to hire and train a new one. However, it is extremely important for top management to keep emphasizing that an employee will not be fired if he comes forward and admits a drug problem, for many workers are afraid to reveal their addiction.

Drug addiction is a disease, not a sin, and the drug problem is a medical and social concern, not a moral issue. This is clearly highlighted by the makeup of the EAP personnel. It is usually run by highly trained health professionals who evaluate the troubled employee, assess most of the medical, psychiatric and social impact of his drug use (as outlined in Appendix B) and order a drug screen for evidence when there is strong suspicion or admission of drug use.

6

Problems With Drug Screening

There are some problems associated with the drug screen:

The donor: Some people will go to great lengths to provide a urine specimen which is not their own in an attempt to avoid detection of a positive sample. It is often necessary to have a witness during urine collection.

The test: There is a possibility of false positive or false negative, especially with the routine procedures. Therefore all positive results are rechecked with a confirmatory procedure such as gas chromatography, mass spectrometry (GC-MS) which is extremely accurate, legally preferred and very sensitive (drugs can be detected for a longer period of time). GC-MS is not used routinely because it is expensive and time-consuming.

The legal and ethical issues: Claims of violation of due process protection, confidentiality and invasion of privacy are often made by employees and union representatives.

While everyone seems to agree on a drug policy, there is occasional disagreement on how to implement this policy. Some labor unions are concerned about the rights of employees. Labor involvement in designing a fair drug policy and labor/industry cooperation in its implementation can help prevent dispute.

The EAP usually refers the troubled employee to an appropriate resource facility while the company pays for treatment as part of the employee health benefit package.

The EAP provides support to the employee and his family while he is undergoing treatment.

The EAP facilitates a smooth transition to work after his discharge from the treatment facility and monitors post-treatment job performance.

By assuring prevention, early detection and treatment of drug addiction, EAP protects careers, keeps families together, saves lives and helps maintain a safe and healthy workplace.

7

Medical, Psychiatric and Social Problems Associated with Cocaine Addiction

Cocaine Impact on Peter's Family

For Peter's family, the picture was similar to the one at his job. He got home late. He hardly talked. He ate little. He "crashed" in bed early. He would verbally, even physically, assault his wife and children, and over trifles. He did not take them out any more. He didn't play tennis, his favorite sport. His sex life was gone; he complained of fatigue and job pressure. His wife started talking about divorce, convinced that he was having an affair with his secretary, ignorant of the fact that he was, in truth, in love with crack.

One night Jenny began to worry when Peter did not show up. It was already 11 o'clock. He had not said, as he usually did, that he was going to be late due to 'board meetings'. Soon after 11 p.m. she received a call from the town community hospital.

Her husband was in the intensive care unit and was in serious condition. She was shocked when she learned that he had an overdose of cocaine and was being treated for seizures and cardiorespiratory failure. Thanks to quick intervention, he was medically clear after nine days and was transferred to the drug treatment center of a nearby psychiatric hospital.

Medical Manifestations

Systemic Effects

Heart and cardiovascular system

Cocaine causes constriction of blood vessels, leading to rapid pulse rate, elevated blood pressure, irregular heartbeats and cardiac arrest.

Lungs and respiratory system

A number of respiratory problems from smoking crack and freebase have been found: nasal congestion, hoarseness, nagging cough with black sputum or bloody expectorates, respiratory distress, exacerbation of asthma and bronchitis. Overdoses of cocaine will cause an increase in rate and depth of respiration, followed by shallow and irregular breathing which could lead to respiratory failure.

Gastrointestinal system

Here complications of cocaine abuse include nausea, vomiting, loss of appetite and weight loss.

Loss of thirst sensations lead to dehydration.

Other symptoms include urge to defecate, to belch, a slowdown of digestion, malnutrition, vitamin and mineral deficiency and protein deficiency.

Central nervous system

Stimulation of the brain may cause tonic clonic seizures manifested by jerky arm and leg movements.

In some long-term users a smaller dose of cocaine can suddenly cause a more stimulating effect because their brains have become more sensitized to the drug. Called the "kindling phenomenon", this can result in seizures.

Complications Associated with Mode of Usage

Intravenous injection

AIDS, hepatitis B, endocarditis (inflammation of the lining of the heart), abscesses, blood stream infection and clots, which can cause pulmonary embolism, are prominent examples of diseases resulting from "shooting up".

Inhalation (snorting)

This method can result in nose bleeds, constant irritation of the mucosa, rhinitis, and erosion and perforation of the nasal septum.

Smoking (crack, freebasing)

Cardiovascular and respiratory complications are exacerbated. In addition, smoking causes impaired pulmonary gas exchange and hemoptysis (coughing of blood).

Body packers

Smugglers may conceal plastic bags or condoms filled with cocaine in their rectums, mouths or vaginas. Some have been known to swallow bags to avoid detection during a Customs search. Rupture or leakage can cause death due to cocaine toxicity, especially via seizures or respiratory arrest. Rupture is particularly likely during insertion or removal of the bag.

Conditions Which Worsen With Cocaine Use

Pregnancy

We do not know yet the full impact of cocaine use on pregnancy. However, since the drug causes a loss of appetite, it leads to inadequate nutrition and a deficiency of vitamins and minerals, thus having a negative impact on the fetus.

Diseases

People with the following diseases are more vulnerable to the effects of cocaine:

Coronary insufficiency, heart disease and angina (chest pain associated with poor blood supply) worsen due to vasoconstriction and a fast heart beat (tachycardia).

Diabetes mellitus becomes more difficult to control because cocaine sensitizes the organism to epinephrine (adrenaline), which in turn raises the level of blood sugar.

Epileptics run the risk of severe seizures due to cocaine's stimulating effect of the brain.

People with high blood pressure face the risk of stroke and heart attack; cocaine constricts blood vessels.

Bronchitis, asthma and lung diseases are exacerbated by smoking crack and freebasing.

Cocaine is broken down in the body mainly by the enzyme pseudocholinesterase. People born with a pseudocholinesterase deficiency might have a fatal reaction to even a minute amount of cocaine. Since the rapid breakdown of cocaine cannot occur, they experience a severe, often fatal toxic reaction. Anyone who has suffered from respiratory distress after general anesthesia or the use of the muscle relaxant anectine may have this deficiency and, therefore, is vulnerable to the smallest amount of cocaine.

Psychiatric Manifestations

Mood Changes

The euphoria which lasts five to 20 minutes is rapidly replaced by the "crash": depression and irritability. There are two other mood changes which may follow: paranoia and psychosis.

The paranoid person is constantly looking over his shoulder, locking his door, looking for people hiding under the bed, afraid that people will hurt him, feeling the police are after him, etc. This may lead to insanity, inducing violent behavior against "attackers", a state similar to paranoid schizophrenia.

Hallucinations, loss of impulse control, confusion and delusions of persecution may lead to assaultiveness and homicidal behavior.

Misperceptions

Auditory hallucinations

Sounds are intensified. There may be ringing in the ears (tinnitus) or auditory hallucinations, such as hearing one's name called.

Tactile hallucinations

Called "cocainebugs", these are described as parasites crawling under the skin.

Snow lights

Snow lights or bright light in the peripheral visual field are caused by changes in the optic system. In addition, there could be complaints of blurred vision and sensitivity to light.

Hypomania

This is a state of restlessness, impulsivity and irritability.

Mania

The user experiences flights of ideas, pressure of speech and distractibility.

Stereotyped Behavior

Picking, pacing, teeth grinding (bruxism) or other repetitive behaviors can occur.

Sexuality

According to many users, cocaine initially increases sex drive and performance. Later on as the use becomes chronic, cocaine becomes the main preoccupation of the users, and sexual interest is lost. Furthermore, there can be problems with orgasm, erection and ejaculation.

Social Problems

At work absenteeism, impaired performance, reduced productivity and considerable loss of profit may result in the loss of employment or business.

At home irritability may escalate into constant arguments, verbal and even physical abuse. This will create a dysfunctional family; a spouse may file for divorce, a child's schoolwork will suffer and so on.

Sociopathic behavior

Values may change. A pattern of cheating, lying, even stealing may develop.

Summary

Addiction is a disease of denial. The cocaine addict cannot see any problem in the deterioration of his physical, mental and social functioning. He does not see that his pattern of using is out of control, despite the fact that he constantly needs clinical attention for the complications associated with the drug.

He may visit a whole range of specialists who may not even be aware that the presenting problem is the result of cocaine addiction. An allergist or Ear-Nose-Throat (ENT) specialist will be consulted for sinusitis, nasal sores, hoarseness and difficulty swallowing. A pulmonary disease specialist may be seen for respiratory distress associated with symptoms of asthma, bronchitis or for frequent nagging coughs of black sputum and bloody expectorates. The gastroenterologist will be consulted for anorexia, nausea, vomiting and signs of hepatitis. The cardiologist will be called upon to diagnose possible hypertension, arrhythmias, tachycardia or angina. The neurologist might check for convulsions, the psychiatrist for depression, psychosis, anxiety and so forth.

8

Causes of Addiction

Drugs have the ability to change the user's mood and to create a temporary state of well-being. Out of ten drug users, perhaps seven will abuse and one or two will become addicted. 'Learning the mood swing', 'seeking the mood swing' and 'preoccupation with the mood swing' are three different stages of drug use. Researchers have been trying for years to identify the etiology of addiction. Now most seem to agree that it is an interaction of psychologic, biologic and social/ environmental factors.

Psychologic Factors

Some believe that addiction is associated with certain personality types. This 'addictive personality' is characterized by weakness, impulsivity, dishonesty and inability to postpone gratification or to tolerate frustration. Although some of these traits are often found among addicts, they could well be the result, rather than the cause of addiction.

Others believe that drug use is an attempt at self-medicating for life stresses, anxiety, depression, boredom and feelings of insecurity.

Unfortunately, when drugs are used to solve life stresses, things often get worse. The person may end up being addicted and thus less prepared to deal with the situation and the original problems worsen.

Social and Environmental Factors

These are primarily responsible for the initiation of drug abuse: peer pressure, dysfunctional family, drug availability, drug-fostering environment, unemployment, idleness . . . However, since not everyone exposed to the same environment becomes addicted, one tends to see a biologic predisposition to addiction.

Biologic Factors

1. Genetics

Most of the studies of the hereditary factor of drug addiction have been done on alcoholics and their families.

First degree relatives of alcoholics are approximately four times more vulnerable to alcoholism than family members of non-alcoholics.

Identical twins of alcoholics have twice the risk of alcoholism than fraternal twins.

The adoption studies done in Scandinavia and the United States reveal that men whose natural fathers were alcoholic have an alcoholism rate four to five times greater than average. This is true no matter who actually raised them — biological fathers or adoptive fathers.

The adoption studies give great credit to the argument of genetic predisposition of alcoholism. There is no reason to doubt that the same may be true of other types of addiction, but this remains to be explored scientifically. Assuming there are genetic components to an individual's susceptibility to a drug, the social and psychological factors remain as contributing agents as well.

2. Biologic Markers

The discovery of endorphins and enkephalins during the past decade has given more hope in the search for a biologic factor of addicition.

Endorphins and enkephalins are narcotics manufactured by the brain. They act like opium, morphine and heroin to control pain. They appear to be created prenatally. It has been reported that endorphins are also found in the amnionic fluid which surrounds the baby as it grows in the mother. Medical use via deliberate stimulation of endorphins goes back many centuries. For a long time Chinese doctors have inserted thin acupuncture needles at specific points in the body to relieve pain by stimulating a surge of endorphins.

As humans experience pain, the body releases more endorphins to enable them to cope. It is speculated that some people are born with a deficiency of endorphin which hinders their ability to cope with physical and emotional pain. Their reaction to heroin, morphine, codeine, Demerol, Percodan and other narcotics is more intense than that of other people.

Based on the same principle, cocaine addicts could be suffering from a deficiency or a slow turnover of dopamine, norepinephrine and epinephrine. Since cocaine stimulates these neurotransmitters, thus creating a state of euphoria, this would probably explain why some people react so intensely to cocaine. Users seem to be saying "Where have you been all my life? You make me feel so good." They seem to get so much pleasure from it because it appears to satisfy a physiologic need.

9

Hospitalization

Hospitalization of cocaine addicts is highly recommended in the presence of life-threatening medical or psychiatric complications, severe psycho-social deterioration and repeated outpatient failures.

Peter entered the Stabilization Unit of the hospital as a corporate executive, devoid of humility and looking down upon the other patients, seeing them as junkies, dregs of humanity. He pontificated as if he still wore the corporate robe.

This is usually a difficult time for the addict. It is marked by anxiety, frustrations about being in such a place, and concern that workplace and friends will learn about this hospitalization.

Meanwhile, with a denial system still intact and operating full time, he keeps minimizing the problem, deludes himself that he can control it, refuses to believe that he needs to be in a structured in-patient setting, refuses to associate his functional, social, familial and physical decline with drugs.

10

Roadblocks to Treatment: Denial

> ***"To know ourselves diseased is half the cure."***
>
> — *Alexander Pope*

Addiction has been called the disease of denial. It is a defense mechanism, an unconscious process by which human beings protect themselves from something unpleasant, harmful or threatening. Denial prevents the addicted person from seeing a connection between his use and his problems, and it can be used in many ways by the addict:

1. He can minimize the problem:

   "I only have a drink or two on weekends; I can quit if I want."

   "I smoke crack once in a while."

2. He can rationalize the problem:

   "I use cocaine in order to lose weight, that's all."

   "I drink only at night because it helps me sleep. A few shots of whiskey can't hurt anyone."

3. He can blame the problem on others:

   "If you were a good wife, I wouldn't be in a bar using drugs and drinking."

   "I don't have any desire to drink. But my friends keep inviting me. I find it hard to refuse."

4. He can become hostile to keep people away when reference is made to the drug:

   "Get off my back. You keep bugging me with your nonsense. How many times do I have to tell you?"

5. The addict resembles someone going down slowly and surely in quicksand; but instead of crying for help, he keeps screaming:

   "Leave me alone! I am in control. I can get out on my own."

The collapse of the denial system is in fact a turning point in the treatment of the disease. However, denial may continue during treatment.

1. **Tap dancing:** The addict continually changes opinion on all issues, confusing the therapist, preventing him from penetrating his wall of defenses and knowing exactly where he stands.

2. **Defocusing:** The addict keeps focusing on everything, every detail except the main reason that brought him for treatment.

   "I really hate this mattress. I need some medicine for my back pain. The doctor is not paying any attention to my ulcers. I can't stand the food. I keep having these terrible headaches."

3. **Playing big shot:** The addict refuses to associate himself with the other patients because of his professional background. He walks around as if he were still wearing his corporate robe.

"I am a banker. I am a lawyer. I don't have anything to do with these people. Hell, no! I am not a drug addict!"

4. **Going through the motions:** Some addicts pay lip service, not antagonizing anyone. They kill time, claiming to be in treatment not because of a strong internal conviction of being powerless over drugs but for a frustrated spouse, an angry boss threatening dismissal or for the judge giving a choice between the treatment center and jail.

5. **Playing the martyr:** PLOM (poor little old me) syndrome (self-pity).

   "No one has ever had to go through what I went through. If it were not for my children, my husband, I wouldn't be using."

   "If my wife were more supportive . . ."

   "If I were not so unlucky; if I were not so lonely . . ."

   The PLOM syndrome is an attention-seeking device which prevents the addict from focusing on treatment.

6. **Knowing it all:**

   "I know how to deal with anger. I know how to deal with resentment. I know! I know! I have been to four programs before."

   This professional patient is unable to realize that the reason why he keeps coming for treatment is because he never learns.

During their first week of abstinence, most cocaine addicts feel miserable, complaining of depression and fatigue. They may become so depressed that suicide is considered. Supportive therapy and close supervision is needed. They experience tremors, muscle pain and severe cravings. Dreams involve buying and using the drug. This physical exhaustion and mental depression is believed to be caused by the disruption of the neuro-chemical balance, the depletion of dopamine and probably norepinephrine and epinephrine.

Neurotransmitters are chemicals connecting nerve cells to one another. It is believed that they play a role in the control of emotions and sensations of pleasure and pain. Cocaine triggers the brain to release a large amount of these substances, mainly dopamine, norepinephrine and epinephrine, which are behind the euphoria. Soon after, the return of these neurotransmitters to the nerve cells for reuse is blocked.

In our research we have found that cocaine depletes those neurotransmitters causing the depression and the irritability which follow the 'high'. We know that a drug named bromocriptine can eliminate the craving for cocaine by making brain cells more receptive to the little amount of dopamine still available until the brain supply is replenished.

As days went by Peter got more and more depressed, spending an incredible amount of hours in bed.

He often had nightmares, dreaming about the drug and waking up with cold sweats and palpitations. He was anxious and irritable, and had difficulty communicating with the nursing staff. He was very demanding, trying to manipulate the nurses and dictate the terms of his treatment. He told them what pills he wanted or should have and when he should have them. At times he refused to take the ones prescribed, such as tryptophan for insomnia and bromocriptine for cravings, despite his initial consent.

Once he began to recover from this difficult period, through education and support, team efforts were aimed at giving him some insights into his addiction and its severe impact on his life.

After two weeks in the hospital Peter felt better and made up his mind to go home.

— I feel fine. I think I have enough tools to stop using drugs. I have learned enough. I am cured. Time to go back home. I have business to take care of.
— Are you giving up before you even start? (nurse)
— What the hell that's supposed to mean?
— Aren't you here to be treated?
— So I am.

— Peter, I want you to know that you are about to be transferred to the addiction unit. That's where treatment will begin. What you have received so far is prerequisite for treatment, a complete neuro-psychological evaluation and lab work.
— What are you talking about, lady?

He angrily rushed to the phone and asked his wife, Jenny, to pick him up!

— Come get me right away. I'm ready to leave. I've got to go on with my life.

To his surprise, Jenny answered very like an echo of the response he got from the nurse.

— But, Peter, are you giving up treatment?
— No, it's over!
— I called earlier and spoke to your doctor. It was my understanding that you would be transferred to the rehabilitation unit soon so treatment could begin.
— I'm tired of hearing this nonsense.
— I'm sorry, Peter, I can't and I won't come and get you. I will no longer comply with your unreasonable demands. You'll have to stay until you are treated.
— I'll leave anyway! Whether you come or not (screamed Peter).
— But not to this house (answered Jenny firmly).
— We'll see!

Peter hung up with a crash.

Her attitude caught him off guard. He could hardly believe that these words were coming from someone who had always complied with his wishes.

Full of anger he went to his room, slamming the door.

An hour later he was transferred to the rehabilitation unit.

11

Treatment

Addiction leaves a legacy. It potentiates or creates a personality with a strong sociopathic flavor. This explains why the treatment of addiction goes beyond detoxification because the disease does not go away by the mere removal of the drug from the body. State of mind, old behaviors and attitudes, lifestyle, must change as well. An addict who is drug-free and detoxified, but has not changed old attitudes and behaviors, is said to be "dry drunk" and it is merely a matter of time before he relapses.

During the days of addiction, cheating, lying, manipulating others, being dishonest, stealing to satisfy an expensive habit, might have been a way of life. It didn't matter what the addict did to get the drug as long as he got it. If you are addicted and you are broke, you will deal, steal or sell your body in order to get money to buy drugs. While in treatment, you must acknowledge, admit, recognize past behaviors and learn new ways.

The staff of the addiction unit is made up of dedicated professionals trained not to withhold feelings and to express their deepest impressions. Among patients and staff a climate of honesty and candor develops. This atmosphere provides the addict with the courage to take an honest look at himself and to learn that the greatest kindness to one another is to be as candid as possible. There are confrontations any time he deviates from staff expectations, any time there is dishonesty, any time he plays a role that jeopardizes his treatment and recovery.

His recovery, emotional stability and growth, is measured by direct observation, by paying attention to what he is saying in individual and group therapy sessions, and his interaction with his peers, by watching his actions and reactions to people and events. The community of the unit is a microcosm of society. The therapist assists him toward a better understanding of himself and a more effective response to living by teaching him non-chemical coping skills.

Peter came to the addiction unit reluctantly, like someone trapped, who has nowhere to go, no alternative. To his surprise the professional team was very friendly. He was well received, called by his first name. He was shown his room. The head nurse gave him a grand tour of the unit while telling him some of the rules and regulations.

However, he felt terrified, tense and uncomfortable to be the center of attention as the other patients quickly noticed a new face. One of them approached him and invited him to join the group therapy session which was about to begin. His anxiety reached a peak since he knew that he didn't have any choice but to join. He slowly took a seat in a corner, head down, hoping that he would not be seen. This was almost impossible since anyone familiar with group processes knows that new members can't go unnoticed.

The therapist started the session by asking him to introduce himself to his peers and tell them the reason for his admission.

"Hi! I am Peter. I was transferred from the Coronary Care Unit of a hospital after I had a heart attack."

Group members, who had been around for a few weeks and who had gone through the same process, quickly picked up his use of denial.

"Gee! It could have been a mistake. You may have been transferred to the wrong place," said Jerry, sarcastically. This was followed by a moment of silence, enough time to give him a chance to catch his breath. Then the therapist went straight to the point in a let's-not-waste-time-playing-games manner.

"Peter, it's obvious you are here for a drug problem. Can you tell the group about it?"

"Well my wife thinks that I have a problem. I drink on weekends, and use cocaine on occasion, but I have an important business and I was working before I came here."

"Peter," said Debbie, "don't bother to defend yourself. We're all addicts. We are here to help each other. Tell us how your addiction affected your job and your family life."

"I don't have a drug problem. I certainly am not a drug addict, and I refuse to talk about myself." Peter was defensive.

He deliberately used hostility to keep people away, but deep inside he was simply afraid to talk about himself.

The group decided not to confront him any longer since it was his first day in the unit. Members of the group focused on other issues during the remaining time of the session.

As days went by Peter slowly began to change for the better. He started to see his weaknesses as well as his strengths. He no longer hid behind his profession. His condescending and patronizing attitude vanished.

He finally recognized and openly admitted that he was powerless over the drugs and his life had become unmanageable. From that time on, the denial system collapsed and he became committed to work hard for change.

During the time he was using drugs, he did all types of despicable things and violated his value system. He then insulated himself behind a defensive wall, and managed to suppress all his feelings: guilt, shame, sadness, anger . . .

As soon as the denial system began to collapse, he became more aware of those feelings which had been suppressed for such a long time. He was encouraged to ventilate them in order to facilitate the healing process. He needed much support as he began to make an inventory of his strengths and weaknesses, and to evaluate the overwhelming impact of his addiction.

"What finally made an impression on me while I've been here in a drug rehab was a series of events which have occurred one after the other over the past few days. My world started falling apart when my cousin killed himself accidentally by cocaine overdose; my best friend got arrested for possession of crack; my buddy got killed in a car accident while intoxicated — he was coming from a party. And then I see my roommate with his legs covered with ulcers after years of intravenous use of heroin. I see a young man with nose bleeds and a perforated nasal septum after years of snorting cocaine. In addition, when I listened to my peers in therapy sessions, I heard my story again and again. I was sick and tired of being sick and tired."

Sobs choked off his words, tears were running down his face when he started talking about the anguish his wife went through, her moments of loneliness and anxiety when night after night, she waited for him to come home.

"I was touched by the whole atmosphere and climate of the unit. I feel a real love here. I have learned the meaning of the word honesty with myself and others. I have learned to be humble. I have learned that addiction is a chronic disease and to control it I must follow a strict code of conduct. I have learned how to deal with anger in a constructive way by either talking to the person toward whom I feel angry or to a third party or to direct the anger toward constructive activities and not allow resentment and ideas of revenge to build up."

Anger is a powerful feeling with destructive impact if it is not dealt with properly. I am sure everyone has said or done something while angry, something they wish they could take back.

Peter has learned not to blame others for his problems. We tend to sometimes point our fingers at others. We must not ignore the fact that no matter what the other person does, we still have to look at ourselves and see how we respond. While it is not easy to change others, we surely can do something about changing ourselves.

During the therapy sessions and lecture series, he was constantly exposed to slogans, most of them from **AA's Big**

Book: Easy does it. One day at a time. Let go and let God. Don't be **Hungry, Angry, Lonely, Tired (HALT)**. No one ever tripped lying down. If you can't go through an obstacle, then go around it . . .

From his own perspective they all boiled down to one thing: In order to recover from his addiction, his life would have to be different.

He would have to get out of the rat race and start moving at a slower pace. He could not allow himself to be overwhelmed by the complexity of life's events. He would have to learn to focus on one problem at a time. Just as one does with a jigsaw puzzle, he would have to concentrate on one piece at a time without losing sight of the whole picture. As things began to come together and the picture developed more fully, he would find himself more in command of the situation.

Addicts tend to see extremes. They often have tunnel vision, seeing everything black and white, unaware of the fact that between these extremes there are thousands of shades of grey.

He learned the importance of assertiveness. From then on he would stand up for his convictions and beliefs, even when it meant standing alone. This applied to drug use as well as everything else. He now knew that the aggressive pursuit of happiness leads to stress; and chemical solutions to life's problems only create more problems.

He was at peace; he had stopped wrestling against himself. He had admitted his addiction. He had accepted the fact that he was powerless over cocaine and that his life had become unmanageable, and that if he had any chance at all to get out of this mess, he had to turn to others for help. He could not do it alone.

This phase of treatment is called surrender or the collapse of the denial system. Without it, recovery from addiction is impossible. It is like overcoming the fear of water in order to learn how to swim.

12

Psychotherapy for Cocaine Addiction

Most cocaine addicts come into treatment when they are subjected to strong external pressures or have serious problems reaching a crisis stage: severe financial, marital or occupational difficulties, or life-threatening medical complications secondary to cocaine abuse.

Behavioral Therapy

The initial phase of treatment consists of identifying the reason the addict came into treatment and using that reason for leverage to keep him in treatment.

The aversion technique emphasizes unpleasant consequences. The addict is taught that things can only get worse if drug use does not stop: divorce, loss of job, revocation of professional license, jail, deteriorating mental and physical condition, etc.

In some treatment centers the addict may be asked to write a letter admitting his addiction and authorizing the therapist to mail it in the event of relapse to an employer, judge, licensing board or other vital party.

Mandatory urine screen is done at least once a week as a deterrent and for early detection of relapse.

Supportive Therapy

The next phase of treatment focuses on how to achieve and maintain abstinence. This is a very important aspect of therapy, taking the greatest amount of time.

In the early stages of treatment trying to help a patient understand his addiction and its impact can be futile. It does not help to spend time preaching the gospel of a clean way of living to an addict who sits in a room all day jittery, suffering from intense drug craving. It is almost as bad as lecturing a hemophiliac on the principles of blood coagulation and how to avoid getting bruises while he is lying on a stretcher with a severe hemorrhage.

In order to maintain abstinence, the addict should be encouraged to avoid the environmental triggers: old drug-using friends, dealers, familiar haunts where drugs are used and drug paraphernalia. He should also be aware of internal stimuli such as feelings of emptiness and boredom that can trigger drug craving. He should be taught what to do in the event of a strong urge to use: Talk to a sponsor or family member, attend an NA, CA or AA meeting; redirect activities; go for a drive, to a movie, to a gymnasium, do anything that can take his mind off the drug. In short, he should take the equivalent of a "cold shower" to cool his urge, and seek others' help if this is insufficient.

The urge to use is caused by the brain's neurochemical depletion, mainly of dopamine, and by a history of conditioned responses. The addiction is permanently established for the remainder of the addict's life. However, prolonged abstinence will cause the urges to use to fade in frequency and intensity. An addict is never cured, but always "recovering" as long as he stays sober.

Another source of supportive therapy are peer and self-help groups, some of the most powerful therapeutic tools. They use the same dynamics that have contributed to the success of Alcoholics Anonymous.

Similar people seeking solutions to similar problems share their individual experiences, confront each other's "character defects", assess each other's old behavior patterns and look at new alternatives, showing a deep understanding of each other's needs.

The secret of recovery lies in the ability to maintain total abstinence and to change one's lifestyle. The Twelve Steps and Traditions of Alcoholics, Narcotics and Cocaine Anonymous seem to offer the blueprint for this new living: a new system of values and a new way of looking at one's self and at others.

At these meetings recovering users lend each other support against temptations to return to drugs and strategies to employ to overcome cravings. Other problems which particularly concern adjustment to a new lifestyle are discussed as well. Feelings of isolation are countered through the friendships extended; abstinence and sobriety are rewarded. In summation, the peer group and self-help groups promote social, emotional and spiritual growth necessary to remain sober.

Developing spiritual dimensions of one's life is also essential to recovery. Building new values or rebuilding the ones that have been destroyed by addiction values, such as honesty, humility, trust, courage, love, sharing and caring come to the forefront. Daily prayers and meditations are helpful for some people, giving them confidence, optimism and inner peace.

Serenity Prayer

God grant me the serenity
To accept the things I cannot change,
Courage to change the things I can,
And the wisdom to know the difference.

The first stage of sobriety is to repair the damages caused by addiction by making amends to the ones who have been hurt, and to let go of repressed feelings, such as guilt, shame, depression, resentment and anger.

Finally, as physical, emotional, mental and spiritual recovery progresses, one begins to enjoy a new way of life without cocaine or any other mood-altering drugs.

Insight-Oriented Therapy

After several months of sustained motivation and ability to maintain abstinence, insight-oriented therapy may begin. The addict should become aware of the needs which cocaine had been fulfilling, and he should learn how to meet these needs without drugs. The user learns to develop and strengthen non-chemical coping skills to deal with stressors. He is also encouraged to find other sources of pleasure, such as social and recreational gatherings with sober family members and friends.

13

Abstinence and Sobriety

The treatment of addiction focuses first on how to maintain abstinence and, second and most important, on how to reach sobriety by improving the quality of life. There is a great difference between abstinence and sobriety.

Some addicts can stop for a while, a day or two or even months especially when they are under strong external pressures. This is called abstinence. But if the addict does not learn new ways to deal with situations, events, feelings that have caused him to use in the first place, he will start using again.

When solid foundations are built on abstinence, on personal growth and development, upon learning new coping skills without drugs, sobriety can then begin.

Abstinence implies the elimination of all mood-altering drugs. Many addicts tend to believe that it only means stopping the drug to which they were addicted. They are not aware of the process of cross-addiction. A recovering person should stay away from cough syrup with alcohol, codeine and tranquilizers. Valium or Librium should not be given to alcoholics after the detoxification period.

Often one hears these types of statements: "I only have a cocaine problem." "I don't have an alcohol problem." "I only have a heroin problem, not a marijuana problem. I can't be in the same unit with someone addicted to Percocet." Cocaine, alcohol, marijuana . . . are like moving from one room to another in the Titanic. A drug is a drug. The brain doesn't care about the name, shape or form. Neither does the liver. The disease of addiction is caused by all mood-altering chemicals, and they should all be avoided if abstinence and sobriety are to be maintained. Cocaine addiction tends to foster the abuse of alcohol, Valium, barbiturates and sometimes heroin. A mixture of heroin and cocaine is commonly used, called a speedball. An addict can be so stimulated by cocaine that he has to use Valium or alcohol to calm down or to get to sleep.

At some point during treatment and at the time of discharge from the treatment center, it's not uncommon to hear an addict pound his chest and say "I'll never use again". Such a statement is dangerous. Overconfidence poses a threat to sobriety. It can invite the recovering addict to adopt a laid-back attitude and stop attending self-help groups, meetings of AA or NA, individual therapy and start seeing old drug-using friends, dealers, places where he bought drugs.

The addict should stay away from these contacts, in person and by telephone, and drug paraphernalia should be destroyed. Seeing them, hearing their voices, talking to them over the phone perpetuates old memories, triggers a desire for drugs, induces cravings. Take this AA advice: "You must change playmates and playpens."

Sobriety is a life-long struggle. It can't ever be taken for granted. Passing the test today is not a guarantee you'll be as successful tomorrow. Take "one day at a time".

Have you heard the story of a 50-year-old artist with a 20-year history of sobriety? During a night of victory celebration he was persuaded to join his friends in a tavern for "just one drink". Hours later, he was brought to the emergency room of a nearby hospital, unconscious. A few months later, he was brought again with severe delirium tremens. In a few moments, he had managed to undo 20 years of sobriety. One drink was too much. One hundred was not enough. The same is true for cocaine.

Some people believe that they can go back to "recreational" use after they have been in treatment for addiction. The answer obviously is a flat no. The road to addiction is a one-way street. One travels from use to abuse; from there one falls into the ditch of addiction. Once this stage is reached, the addict can't ever go back in his life to "recreational" use.

As Alcoholics Anonymous says, "A cucumber may become a pickle, a pickle can never return to being a cucumber."

PART II
Importance of Family Therapy

14

The Family System

From the previous chapters you have learned about addiction and the treatment of the addict. Now let's look at what happens to the family during active addiction and treatment.

For so many of us, the word "family" makes us think of ideal happiness. To those on the outside looking in, the family involved in addiction can look deceptively happy and healthy. In order to understand what happens to a family during addiction, it is very helpful to look at what occurs in any family system.

Each individual has his own personality and role, and will affect other family members by what he says and does. One person's actions will also influence other family members' interaction. The members of a family are affected by additional factors. These can include other family members, work, schools and world events. The family system is a very powerful one, and its members affect each other more than anything else. The reason for this is that these are the people to whom we are closest and care about the most.

Now, let us take a look at the process that occurs during addiction. Previous chapters explained how changes occurred during addiction. These changes affect one physically, behaviorly and in attitude. Family members will be affected by these changes and will respond to them.

15

Co-dependency

The way a family member responds to the changes occurring during addiction will depend upon his personality and role within the family system. Certainly, he will react adversely to the unhappy situation. His feelings may include fear, hurt, guilt and anger. As each member starts to react to the upheaval caused by the addiction, he will start to realize that his reactions are creating no relief. Each person will then start to hide, or repress, his true feelings, and develop a set pattern of behavior to respond to the addiction and to cope with it. This pattern is both negative and harmful.

We refer to this negative way of reacting in the addictive environment as "co-dependency". Basically, everyone in the family is revolving around the addict and his addiction.

Defense Mechanisms

The behaviors adopted by each member of the family are means whereby he protects himself from the reality and the pain that is incurred. This is an unconscious process. The two most common defense mechanisms used are denial and rationalization.

Denial is a common defense mechanism used by addicts. Denial is a process whereby you tell yourself something isn't really happening, or you minimize it. Denial will protect one from feelings of fear, guilt and shame. Most family members feel they are somehow responsible for the addict's problem. They get into a "blame game". One minute, one person will take the blame, and the next minute another is held responsible. Most families will become fairly isolated from society. This is partly due to the feeling of shame and desire for secrecy. Fear exists because of the trauma of the experience, and the feelings of hopelessness and powerlessness it has engendered. These feelings are tucked away and dealt with by denial.

Another common defense mechanism is rationalization. In this process excuses are made for actions. As with denial, this mechanism helps to avoid dealing with one's real feelings.

As an individual starts to build up his defense mechanisms, he develops a pattern of behavior. Each family member will take on a role within the system. Each role will involve a certain amount of ***'enabling'***. Enabling is a largely unconscious method of feeding a problem.

Roles

Initially, a person will try out different behaviors in an attempt to cope with the problem. Eventually that person will settle upon one style, which will become his role. The role adopted by most parents and spouses is that of a main enabler. These entail rescuing, taking on responsibility and arguing with the addict and other family members.

These are means of rescuing or protecting the addicted person from the adverse consequences of his drug use. Enabling is sometimes referred to as killing with kindness. While the intent of the enabler is caring and concern, the behavior is damaging to the addict. It fuels his addiction, it prolongs the agony. The opposite to enabling is "tough love". This approach allows the addict to take responsibility for himself, to pay the price for his behavior.

Enabling has many possible manifestations:

1. Calling sick at the workplace for the addict while he is recovering from his last binge, "the day after".
2. Getting the addict out of jail when he is in trouble.
3. Bargaining with the addict: "If you go for treatment, I'll get you this. I promise."
4. Taking over all his responsibilities: the bills, the landscaping, the care of the kids.
5. Making excuses for his inappropriate behavior: "He is not himself today. He had a rough time at work."
6. Becoming a social recluse by no longer going to parties, movies, church. Not visiting friends so they won't find out about the addiction.
7. Minimizing, rationalizing: "He only uses once in a blue moon. When he uses, he is more pleasant."
8. Accepting verbal and physical abuse from the addict.
9. Collaborating with him: Giving him money to use, using with him.
10. Co-dependency: As explained earlier, this is essentially becoming addicted to the addict. It is the worst form of enabling, and involves engaging in a symbiotic type of relationship with the addict (feeling his pain, becoming part of him).

The children's roles usually vary. One involves excelling in a great variety of positive activities. Another role is the exact opposite. A child adopting this role is labeled a troublemaker, and can become a center of concern, deflecting the family unit from its rightful focus, the addict. A third role is an isolated one. The child becomes aloof from the family, avoiding contact. The final most common role is that of court jester, the child who entertains in an effort at 'comic relief'.

Each of these roles allows its actor to cope with the addiction. It also removes the focus from the addict and protects the addict momentarily. The person in the role attempts to get the problem under control. As things get worse, the behaviors get stronger. As the problem increases, so does the sense of doubt. With doubt comes more feelings of self-blame and questions of what each person must be doing wrong. This whole process with defense mechanisms and roles becomes a vicious, spiraling cycle. It continues to increase with no apparent stopping point.

Helpful Reminders

Remember that the process with roles and defense mechanisms is unconscious. In addiction treatment, there is a saying that "This is a disease that tells the victims that they don't have the disease." The same is true for the family. The process helps them to deny that there is a problem. Each family member also denies that he himself has a problem. On a conscious level, the onus is placed on the addict. The family denies that it has anything to work on.

Another thing to remember is that the roles adopted affect each actor, other family members and people outside the family.

16

Treatment: A Change Agent

When someone first comes into treatment, the family will feel relief. For some it is relief that the person is getting help. For others it is relief that the addict is out of the house and the stress has been alleviated for the time being.

Two misconceptions commonly occur when a patient first comes in for treatment. One is that the addict is the sole problem and that the addict needs to be in treatment alone. The other misconception is that once the addict goes through treatment, the problem will be taken care of and things will get back to normal. Both of these concepts will soon be dashed.

First, the family will discover that the addict is not changing very rapidly, and that the process of recovery is extremely time-consuming. There is no quick fix, no fast-food equivalent for therapy. First, the family had to deal with the addict as a user, and now it is faced with having him totally involved in treatment. The feeling tends to be that things will never get back to normal.

Secondly, the members will start to notice that the stress and behavior at home continues to be the same. Just because the addict gets better does not mean everyone else does. If addiction had brought on a whole new set of behaviors in the family, then those have to be altered individually in order for a person to stay drug-free.

Why don't the behaviors simply go away? First, because there are patterns that are ingrained in the individual's personality. Second, only *we* can modify our ways of acting, and to do so we must know what they are and be willing to change.

There are two reasons why a family may be resistant to treatment. It may not have identified itself as part of the problem. Then there is the fear that occurs as a change in the addict begins to be noticed. The family may not have liked the addiction, but they did get used to it. When the addict starts to change, it may be uncomfortable, especially if the others are remaining the same.

One of the biggest fears is that the reformed addict will leave the family once he is better and more independent. Change is the one main ingredient in recovery, and it is also the one which stands in the way of recovery.

Change will produce, for both the addict and the family, some fear and discomfort. It will, of course, produce benefits in the long run but they are hard to see at first. It also takes time and with all that has been happening, it is hard for anyone to be patient.

Change is also difficult without some guidance and support. It can become much easier with both. The family has suffered. There has been pain, hurt and anger. It is still there in recovery. The family deserves happiness. The question is will the members be willing to take responsibility for change?

17

Treatment and The Family

Encouraging the family in treatment is very important. First of all it allows the family to get immediate support and to feel involved and needed. Secondly, the members have much valuable information and their perception of what has been happening is vital to the treatment process. It is also very important for them to start recovering at a pace similar to that of the addict.

There are three crucial aspects of treatment for the family. The first is the chance to identify their feelings and to vent them. At some point this includes looking at destructive behavior.

The next is opening up lines of communication within the family and the outside world, including the therapist and groups. The family has not only kept their feelings hidden, but they have also become isolated if not physically, at least emotionally.

The third is the need to become educated about addiction and about what occurs within the family during addiction.

How are these areas dealt with during treatment? The most effective and powerful way is to use a group process. Support groups for the family will allow the members to vent freely and to learn that they are not alone. This helps to ease the guilt and to create distance from the illness of addiction.

Separation from the addiction basically means to identify what is going on within oneself and not to be entrapped by the addict's negative behavior and attitude. Multiple family groups are very helpful here. These are groups in which the addicts and their families can share experiences and growth. There is usually a professional present to guide and help in the discussions. Feelings can be shared and people can obtain insight into addiction, promoting openness and honesty. There will be support for the importance of the family in the addict's recovery, as well as encouragement for the family to take care of itself.

Another mechanism in family recovery is work with individual families. It helps the family to look at its unique situation. A family may be willing to talk with a therapist about matters which it would hesitate to discuss in a group. This can be a time of more personal examination of individual's roles and methods of improvement.

In-patient treatment is only the start towards recovery. It allows the family time to stabilize and get immediate support. It also allows much needed space from the addict. During in-patient treatment, the family begins to get basic information and tools to use in the on-going process of recovery. But even after in-patient treatment is completed, the recovery process continues. It is vital for the family to become involved in treatment in order to grow and recover. One of the most beneficial ways to continue treatment is to get involved in self-help groups as a family. The most common of these support groups are Nar-Anon and Al-Anon.

The groups allow the members of the family to get support as well as to look at how the addiction affected them individually. For many it is also essential to remain in professionally led therapy as a family unit.

During the addiction process much damage has been done to the family unit. It has taken a long time for the damage to occur and, therefore, it will take a long time for it to get better.

It will be of the utmost importance that Peter's wife and children continue in group therapy. Surprisingly, marriages which survive the stormy period of addiction, sometimes fail during sobriety when spouse and children neglect to follow therapy or cannot keep up with the maturing personality of the recovering addict.

PART III
Adolescents and Drug Abuse

18

Adolescence: Period of Turmoil

Adolescence begins with puberty, a time of biologic and cognitive growth. It ends with a psychosocial adaptation and the establishment of an independently functioning adult. This period evokes strong emotional responses in the adolescent, his parents and society.

Biologic Growth

The development of primary and secondary sexual characteristics prepare the adolescent for procreation before he can fully understand the emotional implications. His physical maturation subjects him to intense familial, social and individual pressures for which he is not ready.

The awareness of sexual attractiveness in others and oneself, the sex drive and its behavioral exploration and gratifications, the beginning of menarche or menstruation in the female, the first ejaculation of seminal fluids during nocturnal emission or "wet dreams" in the male . . . all of these are associated with the stresses of puberty, causing all types of emotions ranging from anxiety, guilt, shame and disgust to confusion and excitement.

Adolescence is the time for the first emotional attachment beyond the family, the first love affair. "Mad crushes" on movie stars, rock musicians are transferred to a friend or a classmate. These romances bring so much excitement and can turn sour so quickly since they are often broken before the couples really get acquainted. A relationship so fragile, so naive, yet so intense!

Adolescence is also a time of fun, a period of risk-taking, or death-defying adventures. It is a time when one does not seem to get anything from life unless one can enjoy the thrill of playing Russian roulette while parents are on the side line, observing, worried, scared to death of possible consequences.

Cognitive Maturation

The maturation of the cognitive process is also stressful. It opens a new world for the adolescent and for the first time his brain allows him to explore issues that he is not fully ready to understand or that he is able to understand but finds too painful to accept.

From now on he can go beyond concrete reality and is able to think abstractly. Personality development, rights and duties are direct outcomes of this abstract reasoning.

The Psychosocial Process

It is characterized by the emotional and social growth of the adolescent into an independent adult with self-identity. The search for identity and independence is marked by rejection of parental values, the constant assault on parental prestige and authority, and the embracement of peer groups.

This is a time when every parental mixed message is challenged.

"What do you mean 'everyone is equal' when you reacted so angrily that time I came home with my friend Louis because of his (ethnic, religious) background?"

"Why tell me not to drink, when you drink on weekends with your friends?"

This is a time of serious internal conflicts created by the need to distance oneself from parents in order to achieve independence and self-identity while still dependent upon them.

High Risk Adolescents

We have seen that adolescence is difficult even when everything is going fairly well. Tensions arise despite stable family environment, good parenting, decent schools, healthy peer group, uneventful puberty and harmonious development of physical and psychosocial processes of adolescence.

The adolescent can become more vulnerable and less prepared to deal with life when he is exposed to added stresses. These might include delayed puberty, illness and physical deformity creating poor body image and feelings of inferiority. Further tensions might arise from discord between parents, divorce or an alcoholic or drug addicted parent.

Drug experimentation during this period is almost universal among adolescents due to curiosity, easy availability, peer pressure and rebellion. It does not necessarily lead to abuse and addiction, which are signs of more serious problems, but parents should be aware of warning signs.

1. **Mood swings**: Unexplained euphoria followed by sudden and deep depression sometimes leading to suicidal ideations, temper tantrums and impulse dyscontrol.
2. **Change in sleep pattern**: Long hours of sleep in the day time (especially common during cocaine crash).
3. **Weight loss** due to poor appetite and physical exhaustion.
4. **Frequent nagging coughs**, sore throat, nasal congestion, red eyes, flu-like syndrome.
5. **Decline in academic performance**: Behavioral problems at school, lack of concentration, lack of motivation and lack of concern, and "I don't care; I don't give a damn" attitude.

6. **Change of values**: Lying, stealing, becoming sneaky, secretive while money and jewelry begin to disappear at home, shoplifting, traffic violations for speeding or DUI.
7. **Withdrawal**: From parents, isolation from previous friends, going with the "wrong crowd", unfamiliar and new friends suspected or known to be deliquent.
8. **Change in personal appearance**: Punk hairdo, earring in one ear, heavy makeup.

Even when some or most of these changes are evident, parents should not over-react, be judgmental or use scare tactics. It is better to sit down with the adolescent to have an open and frank discussion. If there is strong suspicion, evidence or admission of drug use, seek professional help from a specialist in drug-abuse treatment.

Parents should not see their adolescent's behavior as a reflection of their parental skills and blame themselves.

Children with poor self-esteem and/or poor judgmental skills seem to be most vulnerable. Poor self-esteem is caused by feelings of inferiority (poor body image, feeling of rejection and isolation). Other factors might be feelings of alienation from society, loneliness, lack of love and warmth from parents and a dysfunctional family. Poor judgment skills could be caused by lack of cognitive maturation leading to inability to see connections between a behavior and its consequences. The teenager may suffer from a failure of emotional and social growth leading to immaturity, poor self-identity, lack of goals or meaning to life. Lack of assertiveness may lead to an inability to say "No" to drugs.

Note that the drug becomes a problem in itself, even when the psychosocial stressor that might have led to abuse and addiction no longer exists. Drugs have a physiologically self-reinforcing action.

19

Adolescent Access To Drugs

Factors

In American society access to drugs is facilitated by a number of factors.

Greater Financial Independence

Compare our modern child to his grandparent, who was completely dependent upon handouts from his parents, which were usually hard to come by.

Most children receive an allowance which is increased considerably at adolescence. Part-time jobs add to their income as well. More money and mobility provide greater and more varied opportunities for spending. Tragically, drugs can become one of the consumer products available.

Communication

But what is a parent to do? From infancy onward, the crucial word is "communication" — two-way communication! Talk with your child, listen to your child. Know what he has been doing — out of honest interest. With such a foundation of mutual trust, the parent can usually ask how the money is being spent without appearing intrusive.

What if the parent has only now become aware of the lack of two-way communication? This is a much more difficult situation which may require professional attention. Don't be afraid to seek help, to admit helplessness! It happens to the best of us. Admission of failure is a giant first step, and gets one halfway to a solution.

Rebellion

Compare our modern child to his parent, who sneaked a Marlboro in the restroom at lunchtime, despite his chain-smoking parents' admonition that it would be bad for his health.

Today Susan sneaks a joint, despite her parents' advice to the contrary. After all, she knows her parents occasionally use "recreational" drugs.

While teenagers today may find very creative ways to rebel, the basic outlets remain the same:

- Physical activities (vandalism, theft, sex, racing, neglect of studies, refusing sports teams, etc.).
- Intellectual activities (religion, politics, moral issues).
- Child-rearing issues (nutrition, clothes, personal hygiene, hair).

Of these, the third is the most emotion-laden, most calculated to strike a responsive chord in a parent's heart. Sloppy clothes and weird hairstyles can easily "get his goat". Drug use comes under the category of nutrition, along with our old friend, junk food.

Drugs, since they are so obviously destructive, punish both parent and child. The parent's horror of drugs provides additional motive for the child to experiment with them. He derives triple satisfaction. He hurts his parent; enjoys forbidden fruit and succeeds in punishing himself for being so stupid as to take drugs — a self-fulfilling prophecy. Is this so far removed from the adult who overeats or smokes despite all warnings of the threat to his health?

Curiosity

Like the proverbial cat, the child may not be deterred by the possibility of danger, even death. If drugs are readily available, curiosity may lead to exploration in this area, especially if healthy outlets are not at hand.

Compare our modern child to his grandparent, whose curiosity might have led him to experiment with tobacco and alcohol, since these were sometimes available to youngsters. Drugs almost never were.

His parents had access to some drugs, but modern technology has 'improved upon' their variety and potency.

Parents need to provide opportunities for the expression of the child's natural curiosity in constructive and wholesome activities.

Boredom and lack of self-imposed goals

When Grandma was a child, she knew better than to complain to her mother, "I have nothing to do. I'm bored!" She knew very well that Mama would suggest a dozen chores and make her do them.

Since Daddy was a child, modern labor-saving devices have made the child's help in the house increasingly superfluous. Chores are more a question of tradition and training than a necessity.

Boredom is a companion of curiosity, and directly proportional to the amount of leisure time available in our affluent society. This applies to all economic levels. Very few children must work to help support their families. Even fewer face starvation if they are idle. Work is for extras or for higher education and not a necessity. Spare time, if it is not filled with creative or productive activities, can too easily be frittered away with television, meaningless chit-chat or getting into trouble.

Children without their own goals are at greater risk than those who have at least some positive idea of where their lives are headed and some confidence in their own ability to get there.

Amy, who wants to be a writer, and whose life experience has encouraged self-confidence, spends a lot of time reading. Her school writing assignments are impressive in their imagination and originality. She spends playtime with her much younger brother in spoofs of television commercials and picture books.

Lynn, who has a poor self-image, has only done the minimum expected at school. Her leisure time is spent in aimless visits to her friends, gossiping and walking about to summon other friends. She has no thoughts about her future, does not relate her sociability to any possible career and views schoolwork as unrelated to real life. This will undoubtedly carry over into her adult employment experience.

Peer, Media and Teacher Influence

During the teen years parents take a back seat. The youngster is struggling for independence and identity. The parents are replaced as role models by several sources, namely peers, teachers and celebrities.

What is learned in school and through the media comes into play as well. How a child handles this exposure can be crucial to his relationship to drug use.

This is one area where parental activity and reactions of earlier childhood may have a far-reaching effect. Moral values will be reflected in a parent's supervision of TV shows viewed by a young child particularly if the child understands why a show is off limits. For example, upon reaching adolescence, a child will be less apt to watch a steady diet of violent shows if he has always understood that violence is repugnant.

Propaganda works, at least when skillfully and honestly employed. This has been the theory behind anti-drug and anti-smoking advertising.

Honesty is vital in dispensing such advice. Open communication is a must. Children will listen only to those they choose to listen to, no matter how politely attentive they may seem, and they will listen best to those who listen to them. Teachers and peers are sought out more than parents because of the struggle for independent identity. An internalization of the parents' spoken standards is a prerequisite for withstanding negative influences. *Ipso facto,* hypocritical parents will have a lower success rate. "Don't do as I do, do as I say" should be their anti-motto as they struggle to open and keep open two-way lines of communication with their children, preferably from infancy on.

Feeling High or Relaxed

Lastly, adolescents turn to drugs for the same reasons adults do, to relax or feel high. They are subjected to many pressures, both physical and emotional. They, themselves, may have a limited understanding of what is bothering them, making it more difficult to resolve the ensuing conflict directly.

20

Emphasis on Education and Prevention

Emphasis on education and prevention offers the best way to deal with the drug problem. This must begin at a very early age, even before kindergarten. Parents, teachers and community leaders must all be mobilized.

For any transaction to stay alive there must be supply as well as demand. Goods must be available and people be willing to buy them. In the fight against drugs, there has been more emphasis on control of the supply via interdiction of illegal substances. This approach has not had much success. The supply of cocaine has continued to skyrocket for the past decade. We have been relatively powerless to stem this flow, and its impetus is due to the heavy demand. Just as cigarette-smoking among Americans has decreased dramatically after public education campaigns were initiated so, too, should drug use, abuse and addiction decline if there could be public enlightenment about its destructive effects.

PART IV

Conclusion — Sobriety Pact

21

Sobriety Pact

It was Tuesday morning, Peter's discharge day. He was exhausted and nervous. He could not sleep the night before. Too much excitement! Going home! Reunion with the family! Building healthy relationships! There were good-byes, hugs, kisses, inscriptions in his Big Book as he was about to leave.

A smiling drug counselor shook his hand and gave him this last piece of advice:

"Keep the momentum of your sobriety going. Stroke yourself! There will be instances when you'll be on your own. At a time when almost everyone is using drugs, no one out there wants to deal with a 'straight' person. Some people will make you feel like a dog because you no longer use. Remember that being an addict may not be your fault, but recovery is your responsibility. No one can recover for you. Recovery is a life-long process, a daily struggle, a journey not a destination. One never recovers. One is always recovering!"

Peter nodded gently, acknowledging the wisdom of the words and smiling at his counselor, a man who may have saved his life. He promised to work hard, one day at a time, to keep his ***Sobriety Pact:***

1. He will neither use cocaine nor will he use any mood-altering chemicals. Prescribed mood-altering chemicals must be strictly necessary and supervised by a physician-specialist in drug-addiction treatment.
2. He will not associate with anyone who uses cocaine or any mood-altering chemicals. He will stay away from dealers, places associated with drugs and drug paraphernalia. Selling cocaine, as well as using it, must stop. One cannot abstain while continuing selling. People often find it extremely difficult to give up such a lucrative business.
3. He will enter into the outpatient program recommended by the hospital counselor. He will agree to participate in a weekly urine monitoring program. Random urine drug-screening is used as a deterrent and for early detection of relapse. He will attend one AA or NA or CA meeting every day for the first 90 days and will continue to attend at least two meetings a week thereafter. He will select a person of qualified sobriety (over five years of sobriety) to sponsor him as soon as possible.
4. He will exercise daily, have a proper diet and get enough sleep to keep well and restore the body's neurochemical balance disrupted by cocaine.
5. He will participate in activities that bring satisfaction and pleasure, re-establish relationships with old drug-free friends and will maker new sober friends. He will spend time with his wife and children.

   He will start to appreciate the colors of everyday life, and in this frame of mind, every little thing will give him pleasure: the morning shower, the reading of the newspaper, the first cup of coffee, the drive to work.
6. He will build a strong support system with people on whom he can rely for honest and accurate feedback whenever there is relapsing behavior.

Dramatic changes in his personality structure, his work habits or his social conduct are warning signs of relapsing behavior, preceding a return to drugs. He can turn to this support system for help whenever there is any temptation or compulsion to use drugs. This support system will be most needed when there is a major life crisis: death, divorce, separation, job and financial loss. Situational problems that require major adjustments can jeopardize early recovery.

Peter walked out of the door with mixed feelings of sadness and joy. He was delighted to see a bright sunny day. At a park nearby, kids were playing soccer, some jogging, some throwing frisbees. A cool breeze tickled his face. Life was there waiting to welcome him once again. He felt good. There was a sense of accomplishment. He had stayed the course! He had his life back. He was drug-free. Free at last!

However, he was determined to keep working to remain sober. Recovery is a life-long process, a daily struggle, a journey, not a destination.

Appendix A

Common Questions Asked About Cocaine Addiction

1. **Can someone get AIDS from using cocaine?**
   Yes. Intravenous drug users are at high risk for contracting AIDS, a deadly disease which destroys the body's immune system. Heterosexual or homosexual promiscuity, which tends to go along with cocaine addiction, is another source of AIDS. In the streets now there is a new generation of the so-called cocaine whores, male and female, busy trading sex for crack.

2. **Does cocaine affect sex life?**
   Yes. According to many users, cocaine initially increases sex drive and performance. Later on, as the use becomes chronic, cocaine becomes the main preoccupation of the users, and sexual interest is lost. Furthermore, there can be problems with orgasm, erection and ejaculation.

3. **I don't have a cocaine problem. I only have an alcohol problem. Am I an addict?**

   First of all, alcohol is a drug, a mood-altering chemical. Secondly, cocaine, alcohol and other mood-altering drugs are like different rooms of the same *Titanic.* A drug is a drug is a drug, whether it is a liquid, powder or pill.

4. **For how long will cocaine show in my urine?**

   It will appear for about a week. With the enzyme immuno assays (ETA) and enzyme multiple immuno assay techniques (EMIT), the cocaine is usually detected up to 48 hours after it is used. With the very sensitive gas chromatography mass spectrometry (GC-MS), cocaine and its metabolite, benzoylecgonine, can be detected for up to a week.

5. **What causes the powerful urge to use cocaine?**

   You are touching the very nature of addiction, which involves three factors: compulsion, loss of control and urge to use despite adverse consequences.

   The craving for cocaine is believed to be caused by the brain's neurochemical depletion, mainly of dopamine, and a history of conditioned responses. It takes several months of abstinence, daily exercise, proper diet and good sleep to restore the body's neurochemical balance disrupted by cocaine.

   The addict is also advised to avoid the environmental triggers: old drug-using friends, dealers, familiar haunts where drugs are available and drug paraphernalia. This AA advice must be heeded: "You must change playmates and playpens."

6. **Is hospitalization the best way to treat cocaine addiction?**

   It is highly recommended in the presence of life-threatening medical or psychiatric complications, severe psycho-social deterioration (separation, divorce, job or financial loss), and repeated out-patient failures.

7. **I'm a diabetic. Is it true that cocaine can affect my blood sugar?**

   Yes. Cocaine sensitizes the organism to epinephrine (adrenaline) which in turn raises blood sugar. Therefore, cocaine is particularly dangerous for a diabetic.

8. **I am afraid I have been using too much cocaine. How can I go back to social use?**

   You can't. Addiction is a one-way street. One travels from use to abuse; from there one falls into the ditch of addiction. Once this stage is reached, it is impossible to go back to recreational use. As AA says: "A cucumber may become a pickle, a pickle can never return to being a cucumber."

9. **I have been told that I have a mild form of hypertension. Do you think that cocaine will make it worse?**

   Yes. People with high blood pressure or heart disease should stay away from cocaine. It constricts blood vessels and worsens these conditions.

10. **What are neurotransmitters?**

    They are chemical messengers between nerve cells. Cocaine triggers the brain to release large amounts of these substances, mainly dopamine, norepinephrine and epinephrine, which are behind the euphoria. Soon after, the return of these neurotransmitters to the nerve cells for reuse is blocked. This depletion of neurotransmitters is believed to be the main factor causing the crash, depression, irritability and fatigue which follows the euphoria.

11. **My 15-year-old son has been very moody lately. He has lost a fair amount of weight and has difficulty getting out of bed. Can he be using cocaine?**

    It is possible. The warning signs of drug abuse are:

    a. *mood swings:* euphoria followed by depression and irritability
    b. *change in sleep pattern:* long hours of sleep or somnolence during the day

c. ***weight loss*** due to poor appetite or physical exhaustion
d. ***frequent nagging coughs,*** sore throat, nasal congestion
e. ***decline in academic performance,*** behavioral problems at school, lack of concentration, lack of motivation and lack of concern, an "I don't care; I don't give a damn" attitude
f. ***change of values:*** lying, stealing, becoming sneaky or secretive while money and jewelry begins to disappear at home
g. ***withdrawal*** from parents, isolation from old friends, going with the "wrong crowd", unfamiliar and new friends suspected or known to be delinquent
h. ***negative changes*** in personal appearance.

Even when some or most of these changes are evident, parents should not over-react, be judgmental or use scare tactics. It is better to sit down with the adolescent and have an open and frank discussion. If there is strong suspicion, evidence or admission of drug use, seek professional help from a specialist in drug-abuse treatment.

12. Can my brother recover from his cocaine addiction?

Yes. The disease of chemical dependency is "cunning, baffling, powerful and patient". However, it can be controlled as long as he stays sober. Prolonged abstinence will cause the urges to use to fade in frequency and severity. Recovery is a life-long process, a daily struggle. It requires a lot of work and a complete change of lifestyle because the potential for relapse is forever present.

13. I am a recovering cocaine addict. I have been told that my wife and 15-year-old daughter should get involved in treatment as well. What's the point since they have never used any cocaine?

They should go into treatment. When a member of the family goes through a crisis, everyone is affected. That's why addiction is called a family disease.

There are three crucial aspects of treatment for the family. The first is to identify their feelings and to vent them. The second is to open lines of communication within the family and the outside world. The third is the need to become educated about addiction and about what occurs within the family during addiction.

In order to grow and recover the family members should get involved in individual and/or self-help groups like Nar-Anon and Al-Anon for spouses and Alateen for adolescents.

Surprisingly, marriages which survive the stormy period of addiction sometimes fail during sobriety when spouse and children fail to follow therapy or cannot keep up with the maturing personality of the recovering addict.

14. My wife has been hooked on crack for two years. She has lost her job. I'm about to leave her if she doesn't stop. We are in deep financial trouble. She has consistently refused to enter a treatment program. What should I do?

Addiction is a disease of denial. The addict can be compared with someone going slowly and surely into quicksand but instead of crying for help, he keeps screaming "Leave me alone! I'm in control. I can get out on my own."

The entire family should get together along with a professional in the field of addiction treatment, such as a counselor, social worker, psychologist or psychiatrist. They should confront her on the destructive impact of her addiction in all spheres of her life. They should offer her all the treatment options and the family's threatened responses if she refuses to go along with these options.

This process is called an ***intervention***. The message should be clear and nonjudgmental. Remember, she is sick, not bad; she needs help, not sermons.

15. I use cocaine on occasion. Is there any chance of getting addicted?

Yes. Chances are that you will be, or you may already be.

Each drug affects different people differently. The

variables are: the person, the drug, the amount, the time, the route (oral, intravenous, inhalation), the potency and the situation.

Cocaine is a very potent drug, and when it is smoked, it reaches the brain in two or three seconds. That is why crack, the street drug of choice, gives such an intense and quick high. Anyone who uses cocaine as a recreational drug is playing Russian roulette.

Cocaine can trick your brain, like a con man. While your mouth is dry and your lips chapped, cocaine leaves you dehydrated and tells you that you are not thirsty.

While you are losing weight and your body is being deprived of the most essential nutrients, vitamins and minerals, cocaine eliminates all desire for food and tells you that you are not hungry.

While you need your sleep in order to recuperate and regain your strength, cocaine keeps you awake and invites you to join the party, to be part of the club. Coke Time! Initiation fee, $10 a rock. "I'll meet all your basic needs: food, sex and water. I'll give you happiness, energy and confidence," says Cocaine.

However, what Coke will not tell you is that these "goodies" last only a few minutes, and once the high is gone, all you are left with are fatigue, irritability and depression.

In brief, physical and mental bankruptcy are the 'hidden finance charges' in its price, in addition to tremendous social, familial, marital and economic problems.

Appendix B

1-800-Cocaine Questionnaire

Demographics

AGE	______	ROUTE	______
SEX	______	AMOUNT	______
CITY	______	RACE	______
STATE	______	EDUCATION	______ (YRS.)
EMPLOYED	______ (Y/N)	COCAINE DURATION	______
JOB	______	INCOME	______ 0-10,000
			______ 10-25,000
			______ 25-50,000
			______ over 50,000/yr.

Cocaine History

Started at age __________.
Started with __________ route.
Present route is __________.
Spent $ __________ last week on cocaine.
Do you use: (Choose one)
__________ daily __________ more than once/week
__________ weekly __________ whenever it is available
__________ less than once/month
What was the most cocaine you yourself used in a day:
__________ (gm) __________ (dollars)
Is cocaine your favorite drug: __________ (yes)
__________ (no)
If no, what is? ______________________________
What is the major factor limiting your cocaine use?
__________ cost __________ religion
__________ discipline __________ other (specify)
Have you ever used cocaine almost continuously until your supply was exhausted:
__________ (yes)
__________ (no)
Have you ever used heroin or other narcotics?
__________ (yes) __________ (no)
You called 800-COCAINE for:
1. __________ Information.
2. __________ Help.
3. __________ To help someone else.
4. __________ To check it out.
5. __________ Other (specify).
____

Cocaine Dependence

CHECK AS MANY AS APPLY

Group 1. Negative Medical Effects

1. _____ physical deterioration
2. _____ general health failure
3. _____ loss of energy
4. _____ insomnia
5. _____ sore throat
6. _____ nose bleeds
7. _____ need for plastic or nasal repair surgery
8. _____ headaches
9. _____ voice problems
10. _____ sinus problems
11. _____ runny nose
12. _____ lost sex drive
13. _____ poor or decreased sexual performance
14. _____ trembling
15. _____ seizures or convulsions
16. _____ nausea or vomiting
17. _____ can't stop licking lips or grinding teeth
18. _____ constant sniffing or rubbing nose
19. _____ loss of consciousness
20. _____ trouble breathing or swallowing
21. _____ heart palpitations (flutters)
22. _____ decreased interest in personal health or hygiene (e.g. last MD/DDS appointment __________)
23. _____ other (specify).

How severe do you think these problems are?

_____________ Mild _____________ No real problem

_____________ Severe _____________ Moderate

Has a physical problem caused you to stop using?

_____________ Yes _____________ No

If yes, for how long? __________ (Days, weeks, months, etc.)

Group 2. Negative Psychiatric Effects

1. _____ jitteriness
2. _____ anxiety
3. _____ depression
4. _____ panic
5. _____ fears
6. _____ irritability
7. _____ delusions (false beliefs)
8. _____ suspiciousness
9. _____ paranoia
10. _____ concentration problems
11. _____ hearing voices in head
12. _____ other hallucinations
13. _____ loss of interest in friends
14. _____ loss of interest in non-drug related activities
15. _____ memory problems
16. _____ thoughts of suicide
17. _____ attempted suicide
18. _____ blackouts
19. _____ compulsive behaviors (e.g., combing hair, straightening tie, tapping feet or others)
20. _____ must take other drugs or alcohol to calm down
21. _____ decreased interest in appearance
22. _____ other (specify) ______________________________

Group 3. Dependence

1. _____ think you are addicted
2. _____ real need for cocaine
3. _____ significant distress without cocaine
4. _____ can't turn it down when it is available
5. _____ unable to stop using for one month
6. _____ trying to force self to limit use
7. _____ binge use (24 hours or more of near continuous use)
8. _____ use of cocaine resulting in missing work or rescheduling an appointment or breaking a date or family/social obligation
9. _____ prefer cocaine to talking to friends
10. _____ prefer cocaine to family activities
11. _____ prefer cocaine to sex
12. _____ prefer cocaine to food
13. _____ use cocaine in a.m. before breakfast
14. _____ use of cocaine has led to the need for excuses
15. _____ reduced focus on work and promotion
16. _____ borrowing from friends and family
17. _____ dealing
18. _____ other illicit activity to support habit
19. _____ fear of being discovered as a user
20. _____ usually use cocaine alone
21. _____ Monday absenteeism
22. _____ loss of control over cocaine
23. _____ if you stop using, you get depressed or crash or lose energy or motivation

Group 4. Social and Other Problems

1. _____ arrests because of the drug
2. _____ unusual behavior for you while intoxicated
3. _____ job/career problems
4. _____ loss of job
5. _____ loss of spouse or loved one(s)
6. _____ traffic violations due to cocaine
7. _____ traffic accidents due to cocaine
8. _____ loss of friends
9. _____ fighting or arguments due to cocaine
10. _____ impaired coordination or injuries due to cocaine
11. _____ court case pending
12. _____ loss of pre-cocaine values
13. _____ threats of separation or divorce
14. _____ threats of being thrown out of the house

Group 5. Adverse Opinions

1. _____ people keep telling me I'm different
2. _____ wife/husband/lover objects to use
3. _____ wife/husband/lover objects to amount
4. _____ other important people object
5. _____ feel guilty about effect I'm having on others

Group 6. Finances (As a result of cocaine . . .)

1. _____ in debt
2. _____ no money left
3. _____ used 50% or more of savings
4. _____ caused me to steal or borrow without repaying
5. _____ stole from work
6. _____ stole from family or friends

Why do you continue to use?

_____ for the high
_____ to prevent a crash
_____ for confidence or energy
_____ for sexual arousal
_____ for relief of boredom
_____ for relief of fatigue or lack of energy

Is your cocaine use a threat to:

_____ your psychological health
_____ physical health
_____ relationships
_____ career
_____ happiness

Do you think you ever had withdrawal symptoms when you stopped using?

______________ Yes ______________ No

So far in your life how much have you spent on cocaine

$ ______________

If you had $100 to spend on leisure activities (recreation) would you spend it on (check one):

_____ theater/records/movie
_____ cocaine
_____ going out with friends
_____ going out with family

Appendix C

Resources

State-by-State Guide to Cocaine Abuse Treatment Facilities

(Please note that the listings below are all subject to change).

ALABAMA

Hillcrest Hospital
6869 Fifth Avenue, South
Birmingham, AL 35212
(205) 833-9000
Inpatient

Charter Pines Recovery Center
251 Cox Street
Mobile, AL 36607
(205) 432-8811
Inpatient

ALASKA

Charter North Hospital
2530 DeBarr Road
P.O. Box 89019
Anchorage, AK 99508
(907) 258-7575
Inpatient and Outpatient

ARIZONA

Palo Verde Hospital
2695 Craycroft Road
Tucson, AZ 85717-0030
(602) 795-4357
Inpatient

Sedona Villa
P.O. Box 4245
West Sedona, AZ 86340
(602) 282-3583
(800) 874-9070 (in-state only)
(800) 548-3008 (out-of-state)
Inpatient

ARKANSAS

Charter Vista Hospital
Addictive Disease Unit
P.O. Box 1906
Fayetteville, AR 72702
(501) 521-5731
Inpatient

Riverview Medical Center
1310 Cantrell Road
Little Rock, AR 72201
(501) 376-1200
Inpatient

Addictive Disease Unit
Outpatient Clinic
2700 American Street
Springdale, AR 72764
(501) 756-0412
Outpatient

CALIFORNIA

Southwood Mental Health Center
950 Third Avenue
Chula Vista, CA 92011
(619) 426-6310
Inpatient and Outpatient

San Luis Rey Hospital
1015 Devonshire Drive
Encinitas, CA 92024
(619) 753-1245
Inpatient and Outpatient

Forest Farm
145 Camel Road
Forest Knolls, CA 94933
(415) 488-9287
Inpatient

Alvarado Parkway Institute
7050 Parkway Drive
LaMesa, CA 92041
(619) 583-2111
Inpatient and Outpatient

Dominguez Medical Center
New Beginnings
171 Bort Street
Long Beach, CA 90805
(213) 639-2664
Inpatient

New Beginnings
Century City Hospital
2070 Century Park East
Los Angeles, CA 90067
(213) 277-4248
Inpatient

Merritt Peralta Institute
Chemical Dependency Recovery Hospital
435 Hawthorne
Oakland, CA 94609
(415) 652-7000
Inpatient and Outpatient

Betty Ford Center at Eisenhower
39000 Bob Hope Drive
Rancho Mirage, CA 92270
(619) 340-0033
(800) 392-7540 (in-state only)
(800) 854-9211 (out-of-state)
Inpatient and Outpatient

Alcohol and Substance Abuse Unit
Mesa Vista Hospital
7850 Vista Hill Avenue
San Diego, CA 92123
(619) 694-8300
Inpatient and Outpatient

Haight-Ashbury Free Medical Clinic
529 Clayton Street
San Francisco, CA 94117
(415) 621-2016
Outpatient

COLORADO

Boulder Memorial Hospital
311 Mapleton Avenue
Boulder, CO 80302
(303) 441-0526
Inpatient and Outpatient

Cedar Springs Psychiatric Hospital
2135 Southgate Road
Colorado Springs, CO 80906
(303) 633 4114
Inpatient and Outpatient

CONNECTICUT

University of Connecticut Health Center
263 Farmington Avenue
Farmington, CT 06032
(203) 674-3423
Inpatient and Outpatient

Silver Hill Foundation, Inc.
P.O. Box 117
208 Valley Road
New Canaan, CT 06840
(203) 966-3561
Inpatient

Substance Abuse Treatment Unit
Connecticut Mental Health Center
34 Park Street
New Haven, CT 06519
(203) 789-7282
Outpatient

DELAWARE

Greenwood
1000 Old Lancaster Pike
Hockessin, DE 19707
(302) 239-3410
Inpatient

DISTRICT OF COLUMBIA

Psychiatric Institute of Washington
4460 MacArthur Blvd., N.W.
Washington, D.C. 20037
(202) 944-3400
Inpatient and Outpatient

George Washington University Hospital
Burns Building, 10th Floor
2150 Pennsylvania Avenue, N.W.
Washington, DC 20037
(202) 676-3355
Outpatient

Department of Psychiatry
George Washington University Hospital
6th Floor, North
901 23rd Street, N.W.
Washington, DC 20037
(202) 676-4078
Inpatient

FLORIDA

Fair Oaks Hospital at Boca-Delray
5440 Linton Boulevard
Delray Beach, FL 33445
(305) 495-1000
Inpatient and Outpatient

Coral Ridge Hospital
4545 North Federal Highway
Fort Lauderdale, FL 33308
(305) 771-2711
Inpatient and Outpatient

Recovery Center
HCA Highland Park Hospital
1660 Northwest 7th Court
Miami, FL 33136
(305) 326-7008
Inpatient and Outpatient

Harbor View Hospital
1861 N.W. South River Drive
Miami, FL 33125
(305) 642-3555
Inpatient

Lake Hospital of the Palm Beaches
Star Unit
1710 4th Avenue North
Lake Worth, FL 33460
305-588-7341

Grant Center Hospital
Substance Abuse Unit
20601 SW 157 Avenue
Miami, FL 33187
305-251-0710

Anon Anew
2600 NW 5th Avenue
Boca Raton, FL 33431
305-368-6222

Palm Beach Institute
1014 N. Olive Avenue
West Palm Beach, FL 33401
305-833-7553

GEORGIA

Psychiatric Institute of Atlanta
811 Juniper Street, N.E.
Atlanta, GA 30308
(404) 881-5800
Inpatient and Outpatient

Substance Abuse Unit
Charter Lake Hospital
P.O. Box 7067
Macon, GA 31209
(912) 474-6200
Inpatient

Ridgeview Institute
3995 South Cobb Drive
Smyrna, GA 30080
(404) 434-4567
Inpatient

HAWAII

Kahi Mohala
91-2301 Ft. Weaver Road
Ewa Beach, HI 96706
(808) 671-8511
Inpatient

Drug Addiction Services of Hawaii
640 Kakoi Street
Honolulu, HI 96819
(808) 836-2330
Outpatient

Castle Alcoholism and Addiction Program
Castle Medical Center
640 Ulukahiki Street
Kailua, HI 96734
(808) 263-4429
Inpatient and Outpatient

The Aloha House
P.O. Box 490
Paia
Maui, HI 96779
(808) 579-9584
Inpatient

The Blessing House
P.O. Box 703
Waipahu, HI 96797
(808) 671-3678
Inpatient and Outpatient

IDAHO

The Walker Center
P.O. Box 541
Gooding, ID 83330
(208) 934-8461
Inpatient

Substance Abuse Unit
Mercy Medical Center Care Unit
1512 12th Avenue Road
Nampa, ID 83651
(208) 466-4531
Inpatient

ILLINOIS

Chemical Dependence Program
Northwestern Memorial Institute of Psychiatry
320 East Huron
Chicago, IL 60611
(312) 908-2255
Inpatient and Outpatient

INDIANA

Chemical Dependency Unit
St. Vincent's Stress Center
8401 Harcourt Road
Indianapolis, IN 46280-0160
(317) 875-4710
Inpatient

Chemical Dependency Outpatient Unit
1717 West 86th Street
Indianapolis, IN 46260
(317) 871-3810
Outpatient

IOWA

Sedlacek Treatment Center
Mercy Hospital
701 Tenth Street, S.E.
Cedar Rapids, IA 52403
(319) 398-6226
Inpatient and Outpatient

KANSAS

C.F. Menninger Memorial Hospital
5800 West 6th Street
Topeka, KS 66606
(913) 273-7500
Inpatient and Outpatient

Addiction Treatment Unit
New England Memorial Hospital
5 Woodland Road
Stoneham, MA 02180
(617) 665-1740
Inpatient

KENTUCKY

Our Lady of Peace Hospital
2020 Newburg Road
Louisville, KY 40232
(502) 451-3330
Inpatient and Outpatient

LOUISIANA

New Life Center
Depaul Hospital
1040 Calhoun Street
New Orleans, LA 70118
(504) 899-8282
Inpatient and Outpatient

Jo Ellen Smith Psychiatric Hospital
4601 Patterson Road
New Orleans, LA 70114
(504) 363-7676
Inpatient

Westbank Center for Psychotherapy
4601 Patterson Road
New Orleans, LA 70114
(504) 367-0707
Outpatient

MAINE

Mercy Hospital Alcohol Institute
116 State Street
Portland, ME 04101
(207) 774-1566
Inpatient and Outpatient

MARYLAND

Taylor Manor Hospital
College Avenue
Ellicott City, MD 21043
(301) 465-3322
Inpatient

MASSACHUSETTS

Alcohol and Drug Abuse Treatment Center
McLean Hospital
115 Mill Street
Belmont, MA 02178
(617) 855-2781
Inpatient and Outpatient

MICHIGAN

Psychiatric Center of Michigan
35031-23 Mile Road
New Baltimore, MI 48047
(313) 725-5777
Inpatient and Outpatient

Harold E. Fox Center
900 Woodward Avenue
Pontiac, MI 48053
(313) 858-3177
Inpatient and Outpatient

Substance Abuse Unit
Henry Ford Hospital
Maple Grove Center
6773 West Maple Road
West Bloomfield, MI 48033
(313) 661-6100
Inpatient and Outpatient

MINNESOTA

Hazelden
15425 Pleasant Valley Road
Center City, MN 55012
(612) 257-4010
Inpatient and Outpatient

University of Minnesota Hospital
Box 393 Mayo
420 Delaware Street, S.E.
Minneapolis, MN 55455
(612) 626-5651
Inpatient and Outpatient

St. Mary's Rehabilitation Center
2512 South 7th Street
Minneapolis, MN 55454
(612) 338-2229
Inpatient and Outpatient

Alcohol and Drug Dependence Unit
Station 93
Rochester Methodist Hospital
201 West Center Street
Rochester, MN 55902
(507) 286-7593
Inpatient

MISSISSIPPI

Delta Medical Center
P.O. Box 5247
Greenville, MS 38704
(601) 334-2200
Inpatient

Riverside Hospital
P.O. Box 4297
Jackson, MS 39216
(601) 939-9030
(800) 962-2180 (in-state-only)
Inpatient

MISSOURI

The Edgewood Program
St. John's Mercy Medical Center
615 South New Ballas Road
St. Louis, MO 63141
(314) 569-6500
Inpatient and Outpatient

Alcohol and Chemical Dependency Unit
Jewish Hospital
216 South Kingshighway
St. Louis, MO 63110
(314) 454-8570
Inpatient and Outpatient

MONTANA

Rim Rock Foundation
1231 North 29th Street
Billings, MT 59107
(406) 248-3175
Inpatient

Alcohol and Drug Program
St. James Hospital East
2500 Continental Drive
Butte, MT 59701
(406) 723-4341
Inpatient

NEBRASKA

Alcohol Treatment Center
Immanuel Medical Center
6901 North 72nd
Omaha, NE 68122
(402) 572-2016
Inpatient and Outpatient

NEVADA

Care Unit
Community Hospital of North Las Vegas
1409 East Lake Meade Boulevard
North Las Vegas, NV 89030
(702) 642-6905
Inpatient

Truckee Meadows Hospital North
2100 El Rancho Drive
Sparks, NV 89431
(702) 323-0478
Inpatient and Outpatient

NEW HAMPSHIRE

Hampstead Hospital
East Road
Hampstead, NH 03841
(603) 329-5311
Inpatient

Substance Abuse Unit
Nashua Brookside Hospital
11 Northwest Boulevard
Nashua, NH 03063
(603) 886-5000
Inpatient and Outpatient

Spofford Hall
Box 225
Spofford, NH 03462
(603) 363-4545
(800) 451-1716 (out-of-state)
Inpatient

NEW JERSEY

Fair Oaks Hospital
1 Prospect Street
Summit, NJ 07901
(201) 522-7000
Inpatient and Outpatient

NEW MEXICO

Vista Sandia Hospital
501 Alameda Avenue, N.E.
Albuquerque, NM 87113
(505) 823-2000
Inpatient

NEW YORK

Stony Lodge Hospital, Inc.
P.O. Box 1250
Briarcliff Manor, NY 10510
(914) 941-7400
Inpatient and Outpatient

Bry Lin Hospital, Inc.
Rush Hall Chemical Dependency
Treatment Program
1263 Delaware Avenue
Buffalo, NY 14209
(716) 886-8200
Inpatient and Outpatient

Falkirk Psychiatric Hospital
P.O. Box 194
Central Valley, NY 10917
(914) 928-2256
Inpatient

Regent Hospital
425 East 61st Street
New York, NY 10021
(212) 935-3400
Inpatient and Outpatient

NORTH CAROLINA

Appalachian Hall
P.O. Box 5534
Asheville, NC 28813
(704) 253-3681
Inpatient and Outpatient

Highland Hospital
49 Zillicoa Street
P.O. Box 1101
Asheville, NC 28802
(704) 254-3201
Inpatient and Outpatient

NORTH DAKOTA

Hartview Foundation
1406 N.W. 2nd Street
Mandan, ND 58554
(701) 663-2321
Inpatient and Outpatient

OHIO

Emerson A. North Hospital
5642 Hamilton Avenue
Cincinnati, OH 45224
(513) 541-0135
Inpatient

Woodruff Hospital
1950 East 89th Street
Cleveland, OH 44106
(216) 795-3700
Inpatient

OKLAHOMA

Chemical Dependency Unit
Presbyterian Hospital
707 N.W. 6th Street
Oklahoma City, OK 73102
(405) 232-0777
Inpatient

Presbyterian Hospital
1100 Classen Drive
Oklahoma City, OK 73103
(405) 235-8364
Outpatient

Shadow Mountain Institute
6262 South Sheridan Road
Tulsa, OK 74133
(918) 492-8200
Inpatient

OREGON

Wilshire Psychiatric Group
10490 S.W. Eastridge Street
Portland, OR 97225
(503) 292-9101
Inpatient and Outpatient

PENNSYLVANIA

The Fairmount Institute
561 Fairthorne Street
Philadelphia, PA 19128
(215) 487-4102
Inpatient

St. Francis Medical Center
Chemical Dependency Program
45th and Penn Avenues
Pittsburgh, PA 15201
(412) 622-4580/4511
Inpatient and Outpatient

RHODE ISLAND

Butler Hospital
345 Blackstone Boulevard
Providence, RI 02906
(401) 456-3700
Inpatient

SOUTH CAROLINA

Fenwick Hall Hospital
P.O. Box 688
1709 River Road
Johns Island, SC 29455
(803) 559-2461
Inpatient

SOUTH DAKOTA

River Park Inc.
P.O. Box 1216
Pierre, SD 57501
(605) 224-6177
Inpatient

TENNESSEE

Peninsula Psychiatric Hospital
Rt. 2, Box 233
Louisville, TN 37777
(615) 970-9800
Inpatient and Outpatient

Addictive Disease Unit
Lakeside Hospital
2911 Brunswick Road
Memphis, TN 38134
(901) 377-4700
Inpatient and Outpatient

TEXAS

Brookhaven Psychiatric Pavilion
7 Medical Parkway
Dallas, TX 75234
(214) 247-1000
Inpatient and Outpatient

Substance Abuse Program
Timberlawn Psychiatric Hospital, Inc.
4600 Samuels Boulevard
P.O. Box 11288
Dallas, TX 75223
(214) 381-7181
Inpatient and Outpatient

UTAH

St. Benedict's ACT Center
1255 East 3900 South
Salt Lake City, UT 84124
(801) 263-1300
Inpatient and Outpatient

VERMONT

Brattleboro Retreat
75 Linden Street
Brattleboro, VT 05301
(800) 451-4203
(802) 257-7785
Inpatient and Outpatient

Champlain Drug and Alcohol Services
45 Clark Street
Burlington, VT 05401
(802) 863-3456
Outpatient

VIRGINIA

Chemical Dependency Treatment Program
David C. Wilson Hospital
2101 Arlington Boulevard
Charlottesville, VA 22903
(804) 977-1120
Inpatient

New Beginnings at Serenity Lodge
2097 South Military Highway
Chesapeake, VA 23320
(804) 543-6888
Inpatient

Psychiatric Institute of Richmond, Inc.
3001 Fifth Avenue
Richmond, VA 23222
(804) 329-4392
Inpatient

WASHINGTON

Kirkland Care Unit Hospital
10322 N.E. 132nd Street
Kirkland, WA 98033
(206) 821-1122
Inpatient

WEST VIRGINIA

Highland Hospital
300 56th Street
P.O. Box 4359
Charleston, WV 25364
(304) 925-4756
Inpatient and Outpatient

WISCONSIN

RiverWood Center
445 Court Street North
Prescott, WI 54021
(715) 262-3286
Inpatient and Outpatient

Milwaukee Psychiatric Hospital
1220 Dewey Avenue
Wauwatosa, WI 53213
(414) 258-4094
Inpatient and Outpatient

WYOMING

Substance Abuse Unit
Wyoming State Hospital
P.O. Box 177
Evanston, WY 82930
(307) 789-3464
Inpatient

WHERE TO GET HELP

The following organizations and agencies provide support, information and/or referrals. Starred (*) phone numbers are open during non-office hours.

National Organizations

American Council for Drug Education
5820 Hubbard Drive
Rockville, MD 20852
(301) 984-5700

Cocaine Anonymous Central Office
712 Wilshire Blvd., Suite 149
Santa Monica, CA 90401
(213) 553-8306

Narcotics Anonymous
World Service Office
P.O. Box 9999
Van Nuys, CA 91409
Office: (818) 780-3951
Hotline: (818) 997-3822

National Clearinghouse for Drug Abuse Information
P.O. Box 416
Kensington, MD 20795
(301) 443-6500

National Cocaine Helpline
Fair Oaks Hospital
19 Prospect Street
Summit, NJ 07901
(800) COCAINE

National Federation of Parents for Drug-Free Youth
8730 Georgia Avenue, Suite 200
Silver Spring, MD 20910
(800) 554-KIDS

National Institute on Drug Abuse
5600 Fishers Lane
Rockville, MD 20857
Cocaine Helpline: (800) 662-HELP

Parents Resource Institute for Drug Education (PRIDE)
Robert W. Woodruff Building
100 Edgewood Avenue, Suite 1216
Atlanta, GA 30303
(800) 241-9746

State Drug Abuse Agencies

ALABAMA

Department of Mental Health
200 Interstate Park Drive
P.O. Box 3710
Montgomery, AL 36193
(205) 271-9209

ALASKA

Office of Alcoholism and Drug Abuse
Department of Health and Social Services
Pouch H-05-F
Juneau, AK 99811
(907) 586-6201

ARIZONA

Office of Community Behavioral Health
Arizona Department of Health Services
1740 West Adams
Phoenix, AZ 85007
(602) 255-1152

ARKANSAS

Arkansas Office on Alcohol and Drug Abuse Prevention
1515 West 7th Avenue, Suite 300
Little Rock, AR 72202
(501) 371-2603

CALIFORNIA

Department of Alcohol and Drug Abuse
111 Capitol Mall
Sacramento, CA 95814
(916) 445-1940 or 322-8484

COLORADO

Alcohol and Drug Abuse Division
Department of Health
4210 East 11th Avenue
Denver, CO 80220
(303) 331-8201

CONNECTICUT

Connecticut Alcohol and Drug Abuse Commission
999 Asylum Avenue, 3rd Floor
Hartford, CT 06105
(203) 566-4145

DELAWARE

Bureau of Alcoholism and Drug Abuse
1901 North DuPont Highway
Newcastle, DE 19720
(302) 421-6101

DISTRICT OF COLUMBIA

Health Planning and Development
1875 Connecticut Ave., N.W., Suite 836
Washington, DC 20009
(202) 673-7481

FLORIDA

Alcohol and Drug Abuse Program
Department of Health and Rehabilitative Services
1317 Winewood Blvd.
Tallahassee, FL 32301
(904) 488-0900

GEORGIA

Alcohol and Drug Section
Division of Mental Health, Mental Retardation and Substance Abuse
Georgia Department of Human Resources
47 Trinity Avenue, S.W.
Atlanta, GA 30334
(404) 894-6352

HAWAII

Alcohol and Drug Abuse Branch
Department of Health
P.O. Box 3378
Honolulu, HI 96801
(808) 548-4280

IDAHO

Bureau of Substance Abuse
Department of Health and Welfare
450 West State Street
Boise, ID 83720
(208) 334-4368

ILLINOIS

Illinois Department of Alcoholism and Substance Abuse
100 West Randolph Street, Suite 5-600
Chicago, IL 60601
(312) 793-3840

INDIANA

Division of Addiction Services
Department of Mental Health
429 North Pennsylvania Street
Indianapolis, IN 46204
(317) 232-7816

IOWA

Iowa Department of Substance Abuse
505 Fifth Avenue
Insurance Exchange Building, Suite 202
Des Moines, IA 50319
(515) 281-3641

KANSAS

Alcohol and Drug Abuse Services
2700 West Sixth Street
Biddle Building
Topeka, KS 66606
(913) 296-3925

KENTUCKY

Alcohol and Drug Branch
Bureau for Health Services
Department of Human Resources
275 East Main Street
Frankfort, KY 40621
(502) 564-2880

LOUISIANA

Office of Prevention and Recovery from Alcohol and Drug Abuse
P.O. Box 53129
Baton Rouge, LA 70892
(504) 922-0730

MAINE

Office of Alcoholism and Drug Abuse Prevention
Bureau of Rehabilitation
State House Station #11
Augusta, ME 04333
(207) 289-2781

MARYLAND

Maryland State Drug Abuse Administration
201 West Preston Street
Baltimore, MD 21201
(301) 383-3312

MASSACHUSETTS

Division of Drug Rehabilitation
150 Tremont Street
Boston, MA 02111
(617) 727-8614

MICHIGAN

Office of Substance Abuse Services
Department of Public Health
3500 North Logan Street
Lansing, MI 48909
(517) 373-8603

MINNESOTA

Chemical Dependency Program Division
Department of Human Services
Centennial Building, 4th Floor
658 Cedar
St. Paul, MN 55155
(612) 296-4610

MISSISSIPPI

Division of Alcohol and Drug Abuse
Department of Mental Health
Robert E. Lee Office Building, 11th Floor
Jackson, MS 39201
(601) 359-1297

MISSOURI

Division of Alcohol and Drug Abuse
Department of Mental Health
2002 Missouri Boulevard
P.O. Box 687
Jefferson City, MO 65101
(314) 751-4942

MONTANA

Alcohol and Drug Abuse Division
State of Montana
Department of Institutions
Helena, MT 59601
(406) 449-2827

NEBRASKA

Division of Alcoholism and Drug Abuse
Department of Public Institutions
P.O. Box 94728
Lincoln, NE 68509
(402) 471-2851, Ext. 5583

NEVADA

Bureau of Alcohol and Drug Abuse
Department of Human Resources
505 East King Street
Carson City, NV 89710
(702) 885-4790

NEW HAMPSHIRE

Office of Alcohol and Drug Abuse Prevention
Health and Welfare Building
Hazen Drive
Concord, NH 03301
(603) 271-4627

NEW JERSEY

Division of Narcotic and Drug Abuse Control
129 East Hanover Street
Trenton, NJ 08625
(609) 292-5760

NEW MEXICO

Drug Abuse Bureau
Behavioral Health Services Division
P.O. Box 968
Santa Fe, NM 87504
(505) 984-0020, Ext. 331

NEW YORK

Division of Substance Abuse Services
Executive Park South
Box 8200
Albany, NY 12203
(518) 457-7629

NORTH CAROLINA

Alcohol and Drug Abuse Section
Division of Mental Health and Mental Retardation Services
325 North Salisbury Street
Raleigh, NC 27611
(919) 733-4670

NORTH DAKOTA

Division of Alcoholism and Drugs
North Dakota Department of Human Services
State Capitol
Bismarck, ND 58505
(701) 224-2769

OHIO

Bureau of Drug Abuse
170 North High Street, 3rd Floor
Columbus, OH 43215
(614) 466-7893

OKLAHOMA

Alcohol and Drug Programs
Department of Mental Health
P.O. Box 53277, Capitol Station
4545 North Lincoln Blvd.
Suite 100 East Terrace
Oklahoma City, OK 73152
(405) 521-0044

OREGON

Mental Health Division
2575 Bittern Street, N.E.
Salem, OR 97310
(503) 378-2163

PENNSYLVANIA

Drug and Alcohol Programs
Pennsylvania Department of Health
P.O. Box 90
Harrisburg, PA 17108
(717) 787-9857

RHODE ISLAND

Department of Mental Health, Mental Retardation and Hospitals
Division of Substance Abuse
Substance Abuse Administration Building
Cranston, RI 02920
(401) 464-2091

SOUTH CAROLINA

South Carolina Commission on Alcohol and Drug Abuse
3700 Forest Drive
Columbia, SC 29204
(803) 758-2521 or 758-2183

SOUTH DAKOTA

Division of Alcohol and Drug Abuse
Joe Foss Building
523 East Capitol
Pierre, SD 57501
(605) 773-3123

TENNESSEE

Alcohol and Drug Abuse Services
Tennessee Department of Mental Health and Mental Retardation
James K. Polk Building
505 Deaderick Street
Nashville, TN 37219
(615) 741-1921

TEXAS

Drug Abuse Prevention Division
Texas Department of Community Affairs
2015 South IH 35
Austin, TX 78741
(512) 475-2311

UTAH

Division of Alcoholism and Drugs
150 West North Temple, Suite 350
P.O. Box 2500
Salt Lake City, UT 84110
(801) 533-6532

VERMONT

Alcohol and Drug Abuse Division
103 South Main Street
Waterbury, VT 05676
(802) 241-2170 or 241-1000

VIRGINIA

State Department of Mental Health and Mental Retardation
P.O. Box 1797
109 Governor Street
Richmond, VA 23214
(804) 786-5313

WASHINGTON

Bureau of Alcoholism and Substance Abuse
Washington Department of Social and Health Services
Mail Stop OB-44W
Olympia, WA 98504
(206) 753-5866

WEST VIRGINIA

Division of Alcohol and Drug Abuse
State Capitol
1800 Washington Street, East, Room 451
Charleston, WV 25305
(304) 348-2276

WISCONSIN

Office of Alcohol and Other Drug Abuse
1 West Wilson Street
P.O. Box 7851
Madison, WI 53705
(608) 226-3442

WYOMING

Alcohol and Drug Abuse Programs
Hathaway Building
Cheyenne, WY 82002
(307) 777-7115, Ext. 7118

PUERTO RICO

Department of Addiction Control Services
Box B-Y, Rio Piedras Station
Rio Piedras, PR 00928
(809) 763-5823

VIRGIN ISLANDS

Division of Mental Health, Alcoholism and Drug Dependency
P.O. Box 7309
St. Thomas, VI 00801
(809) 774-4888

Bibliography

Brunstetter, R.W.; Silver, L.B. **Normal Adolescent Development**, Comprehensive Textbook of Psychiatry Volume II, Fourth Edition by Kaplan H. & Sadock B. Baltimore: Williams and Wilkins, 1985.

Burglass, S. **The Success Syndrome**. New York: Plenum, 1986.

Cohen, S. **Cocaine, Acute Medical and Psychiatric Complications.** *Psychiatric Annals* 14(10) 728-732, 1984.

Dackis, C.A.; Gold M.S. **Bromocriptine as Treatment of Cocaine Abuse.** *The Lancet* 1151-52, May 18, 1985.

New Concepts in Cocaine Addiction: The Dopamine Depletion Hypothesis. *Neuroscience & Behavioral Reviews,* Vol 9: 469-77, 1985.

Facklan, M. & H. **The Brain: Magnificent Mind Machine**. New York: Harcourt Brace Javanovich, 1982.

Flax, S. **The Executive Addict**. *Fortune Magazine,* June 24, 1985.

Gold, M.S.; Dackis, C.A. **Role of Laboratory in the Evaluation of Suspected Drug Abuse.** *Journal of Clinical Psychiatry.* Volume 47(1), January, 1986.

Gold, M.S. **800-Cocaine.** New York: Bantam Books, 1984.

Gold M.S. **The Facts About Drugs and Alcohol**. New York: Bantam Books, 1986.

Khantzian, E.J.; Khantzian, N.J. **Cocaine Addiction: Is There a Psychological Predisposition?** *Psychiatric Annals* 14(10): 753-59, 1984.

MacDonald, D.I. **Drugs, Drinking and Adolescents.** Chicago: Year Book Medical Publishers, 1984.

Maxwell, R. **Breakthrough: What to Do When Alcohol or Chemical Dependency Hits Close to Home.** New York: Ballantine Books, 1986.

Merryman, R. **Broken Promises, Mended Dreams.** New York: Berkley Books, 1984.

Schuckit, M.A. **Drug and Alcohol Abuse, 2nd Edition.** New York: Plenum Press, 1984.

Smith, D.E.; Wesson, D.R. **Treating the Cocaine Abuser.** Center City, Minn: Hazelden, 1985.

Wegscheider, S. **Another Chance: Hope and Health for the Alcoholic Family.** California: Science and Behavior Books, 1981.

Weiss, R.D.; Merin, S.M. **Cocaine.** Washington, D.C.: American Psychiatric Press, 1986.

Wilford, B.B. **Drug Abuse: A Guide for the Primary Care Physician.** Chicago: American Medical Association, 1981.